# Middle East in Crisis & Conflict

TAUFIQ RAHIM

# Middle East in Crisis & Conflict

## A PRIMER

2040 WORLD

Middle East in Crisis and Conflict: A Primer
© 2024, Taufiq Rahim. All rights reserved.

Published by 2040 World, New York, N.Y. 10001

ISBN 979-8-9901347-1-3 (paperback)
ISBN 979-8-9901347-0-6 (eBook)

Publisher's Cataloging-in-Publication
(Provided by Cassidy Cataloguing Services, Inc.)

Names:      Rahim, Taufiq, author.
Title:    Middle East in crisis & conflict : a primer / Taufiq Rahim.
Other titles:    Middle East in crisis and conflict
Description:    New York, N.Y. : 2040 World, [2024]
Identifiers:    ISBN: 979-8-9901347-1-3 (paperback) | 979-8-
                9901347-0-6 (ebook) | LCCN: 2024904262
Subjects:    LCSH: Middle East--History--21st century. | Middle
                East--Foreign relations--21st century. | Middle East--
                Politics and government--21st century. | Arab-Israeli
                conflict--21st century. | BISAC: POLITICAL SCIENCE
                / World / Middle Eastern. | POLITICAL SCIENCE /
                International Relations / Diplomacy. | HISTORY /
                Middle East / Israel & Palestine.
Classification:    LCC: DS63.123 .R34 2024 | DDC: 956.054--dc23

To request additional permissions or for general inquiries, contact
print@2040.world

# CONTENTS

# PREFACE

Since the attacks by Hamas in Israel's Southern District on Saturday, October 7, 2023, there has been both a feeling and reality of escalating, if not spiraling, conflict and crisis in the Middle East. Faced with an overflow of news, images, and social media, it is hard to understand it all. Fundamentally, the situation is deeply personal for many. And there are far-reaching political implications. Beyond all this, moral considerations are at the core.

This primer seeks to distill the information, insights, and implications necessary to help observers and experts alike navigate the present crisis and conflict in the Middle East. It is a window into a much wider body of facts and opinions. Each reader must do the broader work to learn more and build an informed perspective.

This publication is not meant to be a political extract. Words are used not according to partisan persuasion or to align with any technical jargon but according to common usage. Palestine is used at times, as is Palestinian territories, and the word *occupied* is used instead of *disputed* where relevant. Likewise, the term *terrorist* is, at times, used instead of *militant*.

This edition was last updated on February 26, 2024. Given the speed and intensity to ensure publication, there may be limited missteps in dates, titles, formal names, and minor details. Subsequent editions will endeavor to correct what is required. In addition, given the fast-moving situation, readers will need to incorporate the latest news and developments into their understanding of the conflict. Notably, it appears discussions are in advanced stages for a framework for a hostage deal that could lead to an interim ceasefire.

Finally, the dispassionate nature of this writing does not seek to avoid the humanitarian nature of the current situation. May better times be ahead for all.

# I

# UP FRONT

Before delving into the details, here is the framing up front:

- The terrorist attacks on October 7, 2023, by Hamas represented the greatest loss of Jewish life in one day since the Holocaust.

- The Gaza Strip ("Gaza") has faced an unprecedented bombardment by Israel and a subsequent humanitarian crisis beginning the same day.

- These events are part of a complex history—wars, displacement, occupation, intersecting relationships, and long memories—before even 1948.

- Various fronts in Lebanon, Syria, Iraq, and Yemen have remained flashpoints that could further ignite.

- The United States has played the lead role in the international community's response, although efforts for de-escalation have been largely ineffective.

- Other countries, notably South Africa, have leveraged various international forums to call attention to the conflict.

- The crisis in the Middle East has set alight the political scene in Europe and North America in a way that will affect domestic alignment across left and right.

- While contagion to the Gulf has been contained, and the same is largely true for global energy markets, this may change if the conflict extends further into mid-2024.

- More critically, the world faces two significant conflicts with global power dimensions (Ukraine and now Gaza); a third could rock the geopolitical map and cause tectonic issues for supply chains, economies, and travel.

- Private organizations may be tempted to take political stands but should take humanitarian ones.

- Individuals may not know where to turn for news, input, or insights. Things that seem clear one day may not be the next. All should consider and speak carefully.

# II

# QUESTIONS & ANSWERS

## 1. What are the latest developments (as of February 26, 2024)?

The death toll continues to climb, reaching, by the date of publication, over 1,400 on the Israeli side and 30,000 on the Palestinian side. This includes both civilian and military casualties. While the direct conflict has primarily taken place in the Gaza Strip, fighting has spread to the West Bank, and there have been ongoing tit-for-tat skirmishes between forces in southern Lebanon and northern Israel. Israel mandated the mass evacuation of Palestinians from almost all urban centers of Gaza during its ground incursions.

The unprecedented bombardment by Israel has led to damage to civilian infrastructure in some areas at a level—statistically—not seen since World War II. The humanitarian crisis in Gaza also has raised alarm bells across the world. Israel, which had been primarily responsible for enabling water and fuel provision in the Strip, has either entirely or intermittently cut off supplies. It has also disrupted telecommunications networks.

While the United Nations has fully mobilized, and many organizations have responded to calls for aid, ongoing restrictions limit the ability of trucks with needed supplies to cross into Gaza. Several organizations are tracking the humanitarian situation daily, such as Anera (www.anera.org). Egypt, in coordination with the United States and Israel, has intermittently opened the Rafah border crossing to allow the evacuation of foreign citizens and relatives and the entry of limited supplies.

There has been continued rocket fire, albeit with declining frequency, from the Gaza Strip into all parts of Israel since October 7, 2023. At times, hundreds of rockets have been fired by Hamas daily, an accumulation that already exceeds prior rounds of conflict. It was previously thought that Hamas did not have such a large arsenal in terms of quantity and quality. Israel has launched airstrikes with an intensity that outpaces the American campaigns in Iraq and Afghanistan.

Of the estimated 250 hostages, around 130 remain under Hamas (and some affiliated groups) control at the time of publication. It is assumed, and Hamas has asserted, that the Israeli bombardment has led to the deaths of several of these hostages. How many others have been directly harmed by Hamas during their captivity is unknown, as Hamas has denied access to the International Committee of the Red Cross (ICRC) or any other body.

Negotiations primarily led by Qatar resulted in an initial release of hostages in exchange for Palestinian prisoners held by Israel. The hostages released consisted of women, children, and some foreign nationals. The ones that remain in captivity are predominantly Israeli soldiers, although a number of civilians (including children) and foreign nationals continue to be held. Within Israel, the number of Palestinians held as prisoners has grown due to the recent offensive in Gaza and is upwards of 10,000. How many of them are civilians versus militants will be a matter of intense debate.

Diplomatically, many officials have traveled to the region since the crisis began. In the initial days, this included the leadership of the European Union, U.S. President Joe Biden, and leading officials from Canada, the United Kingdom, and Germany. Subsequently, U.S. Secretary of State Anthony Blinken was notably engaged across the region, especially in Qatar, Jordan, Egypt, the United Arab Emirates, and Turkey. The priorities have been opening a humanitarian corridor, strengthening the hostage negotiations, and fostering what have been called "humanitarian pauses." Beginning in 2024, there have been increasing efforts for a comprehensive deal to bring the current war to an end.

There has been growing anxiety in Israel due to the continued plight of hostages, contributing to sustained anger towards Hamas and Palestinian authorities, but also directed at the Israeli government itself, which, while in a somewhat unity government formation (without the principal opposition leader partaking), has remained unpopular. In the Palestinian territories and the surrounding Arab world, sentiment has dramatically intensified, primarily on social media. The size of demonstrations in places such as Baghdad in the initial days was significant. Recent demonstrations have been relatively contained across the Arab and Muslim world.

The political polarization and charged atmosphere of past years in Europe and North America have come to affect reactions to the crisis in Western capitals. Protests and counter-protests are abundant, as are inflammatory rhetoric, government warnings, and rising hate crimes. It is, all in all, a multifaceted situation, evolving day-by-day, with political positions changing with each development.

Overall, hostilities have already spread as far afield as the Red Sea. The situation in Iraq is particularly volatile as it involves a number of disparate paramilitary forces testing the responses of the U.S. military in the country. What many are watching for is whether the conflict will grow to become a full-scale regional war beyond the boundaries of Israel and Palestine.

Thus far, attempts have been made to avoid this, notably by Iran and America towards one another directly. It is nevertheless a tinderbox. The incident in late January along the Jordanian-Syrian border targeting the American military base, Tower 22, was particularly worrying and raised tensions significantly. Further strikes by Iranian proxy forces in the region leading to significant U.S. military casualties could set everything alight.

It is easy to understate the situation that has unfolded in the Gaza Strip since October 7, 2023. Imagine if all of Tel Aviv, Israel's largest city, had been systematically bombed, every single resident marched out, and thousands of children killed. That is what has happened in Gaza City, the largest Palestinian city. Whether this is justified or proportionate is politically debated; however, objectively, this has become the reality on the ground.

That reality in Gaza City has been replicated to varying degrees in almost every urban center in the Gaza Strip. In addition to the deaths, upwards of 50,000 Palestinians (and rising) representing two percent of the population have been injured, and nearly 75% of the population, if not more, has been displaced. Hundreds of thousands had become food insecure by early 2024.

Finally, the fog of war is alive and well, and claims and counterclaims abound, particularly regarding the full nature of the October 7 attacks and the more egregious casualty events in the Gaza Strip. These discussions are somewhat irrelevant. The Hamas assault was barbaric. Israel is killing countless civilians systematically. No one story can change that. Unfortunately, parsing details from thousands of miles away is a fruitless exercise in the fog of war.

What will prove pivotal is a significant escalating event in which propaganda may incite a broadening of the conflict.

## 2. How did this recent crisis start?

This recent crisis started with the assault by Hamas, which controls the Gaza Strip and administers the government there. That assault was unprecedented in its nature, scope, and loss of life in the entire history of the conflict for the Israeli side. This event, of course, cannot be disentangled from the broader situation and interconnected conflict that now spans decades.

The Hamas incursion was carried out in a very calculated way on October 7, 2023, 50 years to the day of the start of the Yom Kippur War, which is considered within Israel as the most significant military failure in its history. In that war, the national armies of Syria and Egypt launched a surprise attack, which, while eventually repelled, forced Israel to the negotiation table for the first time and resulted in significant military casualties and damage. Only through American resupply of munitions and military equipment did Israel regain the upper hand in that conflict. It led to the eventual resignation of Israeli Prime Minister Golda Meir.

The October 7 operation required careful planning given its scope, estimated to go back at least two years. That would mean, while ongoing factors were exacerbating the situation, this act was pre-planned and fully intended by Hamas to occur. The planning would have also required significant materials and technological support. While this would have come from Iran, it is unclear to what extent they played a part in operational planning. There also appeared to be other military capabilities deployed that were previously not thought to have been possessed by Hamas. Did this come from Russia? The black market? Former ISIS fighters? This is not yet clear.

The assault itself was sustained and multi-pronged. It continued for seven hours without much interruption, which has raised significant questions and red flags related to the failures on the Israeli side. There was a complete breakdown due to Israel's political situation, with street protests aggressively challenging the government in the weeks before the attacks. The government and intelligence services had a severe communication issue as a result. After the attacks, it has been alleged that there may have been warnings about a pending operation that were either ignored, missed, or dismissed.

Much has already been written about the nature of the October 7 attacks, and the details are described well in a number of news publications. However, it is essential to understand some aspects that have created a new national trauma in Israel. Here is a brief overview of what happened:

- **Rockets** — Hamas and other groups coordinating with it launched a barrage of rockets, numbering between 3,000–5,000, primarily toward Israel's Southern District; concurrently, a public statement announced 'Operation Al Aqsa Flood' had begun.

- **Paragliders** – An unknown number of Hamas militants used motorized paragliders to fly into Israel, including towards a rave, where there were estimated to be hundreds of casualties.

- **Border incursions** – Both Hamas and plainclothes partisans (maybe to be used as an excuse later to sidestep responsibility) crossed through the border fence, which explosions and bulldozers in certain areas had partially dismantled.

- **Marine landing** – At Zikim, there was a marine landing of several boats from Gaza that also facilitated the incursion of militants, who then went deeper into Israeli territory.

- **Massacre at rave** – Many young people were hunted down as they hid and ran. Many of the initial hostages were attendees of the rave, which was held near the border. Given the nature of the assault, it appears that this was a planned mass casualty event by Hamas, although others contest this.

- **Raids on local areas** – Organized raids were carried out against local towns (Sderot, Ofakim), *kibbutzim* or *moshavim* (Kfar Aza, Nir Oz, Be'eri, Magen, Sufa, Nahal Oz, and Netiv Haasara), and military bases (Bahad 4, Re'im), many of which fell temporarily under the control of Hamas.

These were mass casualty events, but attention was given to ensuring hostages were taken. There is an evolving body of facts regarding physical and sexual abuses carried out during the raids. Significant battles also occurred in beach areas, police stations, and street-to-street. Military hostages in particular, who represent an unknown number of the total, are being used as leverage to release Palestinian prisoners held by Israel in ongoing negotiations.

Throughout the overall assault, Hamas also damaged houses and vehicles and left fighters behind for continued skirmishes (and who knows what else). The group absconded by the end of the day with around 250 hostages brazenly across the border. The best overall map of the day's incidents is captured at oct7map.com.

On that long Saturday, although the Israeli government was still in disarray, a counterattack and assault on Gaza started in the evening and has continued since, mainly from the air.

## 3. What was the other immediate context?

These events, of course, did not take place in a vacuum. Several contemporaneous developments should be noted.

- **Netanyahu government** – Before the recent round of hostilities, the government led by Prime Minister Benjamin Netanyahu was in peril after nine months of street protests. It was deeply unpopular, facing significant issues from the American Jewish diaspora and related organizations and even pressure from the Biden administration. Whether it would fall or not was unclear, but for the first time, perhaps existential divisions were appearing in Israel.

- **Abraham Accords** – The Abraham Accords, first seen as a sideshow by some mainstream commentators, took a very central role in the discussion of the conflict. While the United Arab Emirates, Bahrain, and Morocco were not necessarily parties to the conflict, the agreements were seen as shifting the dynamic of the region. The question, though, was, would Palestinians be the afterthought?

The Accords focused on economic and security interests, and offered nothing tangibly to be gained for the Palestinians themselves. That seemed to be in the interests of Israel, as it would be able to maintain the status quo in the occupied territories and still expand relations in the Arab World.

The talks in mid-2023 with the Kingdom of Saudi Arabia around normalization, facilitated by the Biden administration, were very advanced. Interestingly, Saudi Arabia moved the Palestinian issue closer to the forefront. This was an irritant to both the Netanyahu government and perhaps Hamas. For Israel, the purpose of Gulf normalization was to 'skip' normalization on the Palestinian issue. For Hamas, any deal with Saudi Arabia that addressed the Palestinian issue would empower its rivals in Fatah and the Palestinian Authority.

• **Iran–Saudi rapprochement** – During the pandemic, there was an uptick in conversations between Iran and Gulf states soon after Biden took office. Realizing that the Biden administration would seek to bring the Iran deal back in some form, the Gulf states sought to alter the strategic threat from Iran through direct engagement. This initially involved the UAE, and then Saudi Arabia, through mediation by China, had a breakthrough with Iran. Today, there are normalized– not perfect–relations between the two parties. In fact, during the recent crisis, the first-ever call was held between Crown Prince Mohammed bin Salman and the President of Iran, Ebrahim Raisi, followed soon after by an in-person meeting.

• **The situation in the Palestinian territories** – The situation in the Palestinian territories has remained volatile, and in the months prior to the October 7 attacks, there were exacerbating tensions, notably in the West Bank. Also, in East Jerusalem, which is under full Israeli administration, there were rising clashes. While the Palestinian territories can always seem restive, it appeared that the Palestinian Authority in the West Bank was anemically moving along and that Hamas was 'quiet' on the Gaza front.

As for the overall status quo on the ground, it should be clear that the Israeli government continued to control almost all aspects of the West Bank with an ever-expanding settlement presence. The Palestinian Authority effectively administers municipal areas in parts of the West Bank. In the Gaza Strip, from a day-to-day scenario, Hamas has had administrative control (in municipalities). The border with Egypt, Rafah, has strict procedures but, in some respects, represents an 'international' border for Gaza; the Erez Crossing with Israel was being opened semi-frequently for limited purposes.

The slow suffocation of the occupation and siege are hard to capture, as they are not sudden events. Instead, there is a day-to-day accumulation of humiliations, checkpoints, confiscations, house demolitions, harassment incidents, arrests, shootings, and overall deprivation. The Israeli NGO B'Tselem regularly documents this slow accumulation of incidents on its website (www.btselem.org). While there had been relative quiet in the sense of no active conflict, it was by no means a resolved situation.

- **Role of Hamas** – Since the Netanyahu government came to power, and since the last 2021 round of fighting, the status quo with Hamas was holding. Hamas had maintained its leadership in Doha and was publicly focused on economic issues. In coordination with the Israeli government, the number of work permits had increased to close to 20,000. There was no visible indication that an escalation was afoot.

In 2023, before October 7, total casualties had reached over 200 in the Palestinian territories, with a large share in the West Bank. There were some notable rounds of rocket fire and Israeli airstrikes in Gaza, mostly involving Palestinian Islamic Jihad. Overall, from a military standpoint, the situation was relatively quiet. However, there was a rising feeling that the status quo was at a breaking point, given the lack of discernible process towards any improvement of the Palestinian situation. That it would lead to the dramatic attacks on October 7, 2023 was nevertheless a shock.

## 4. How exactly does Hamas function, and what is the role of Iran specifically?

Hamas as a group has been around for decades, first as a religious-social group, then a religious-social-political group, then a religious-social-political-military group, and then eventually the governing authority in the Gaza Strip. It has maintained its regional apparatus, which operates not just in Gaza but also in the West Bank and within Palestinian refugee camps in Lebanon. In addition, it has a political bureau in Qatar, a smaller office in Turkey, and a multifaceted station in Iran. The military wing is called the Izz Ad-Din Al Qassam Brigades.

Hamas has an unknown set of representatives in some other countries, which both Israel and the United States are broadly aware of. Its links with China and Russia are murky and often channeled through Iran. Russia never developed closer operational ties with Hamas as it did with Hezbollah during the Syrian conflict. Hezbollah separately has a tie-up with Hamas that is coordinated in many ways through representatives in Lebanon.

Despite Hamas's opposition to Syrian President Bashar Al Assad during the height of the civil war in Syria, a country where it had previously very close ties as part of the so-called 'resistance' axis, it has since mended ties. In the last several years, Hamas has tried to have an open relationship with all parties within the region.

The détente between Iran and Saudi Arabia enabled a Hamas delegation to visit Saudi Arabia in 2023, the first such visit in many years. It can be assumed that there is a direct and ongoing set of conversations currently between many Arab countries and Hamas. Egypt, due to the border with Gaza and the militants present in Sinai, closely coordinates with Hamas on ongoing security matters.

While, in 2006, Hamas won control of the Palestinian legislature and ostensibly became the governing authority, the following year's civil strife effectively removed the group from primacy in the West Bank; Hamas was subsequently politically marginalized from the scene in the West Bank. The movement was never integrated into the broader Palestine Liberation Organization (PLO), and since 2006, there has neither been a presidential nor parliamentary election of the Palestinian Authority (PA). Hamas, therefore, had de facto but not de jure status in representing Palestinians in Gaza.

In addition to its rule in Gaza, Hamas essentially has provenance over armed resistance within Palestinian factions, who generally defer to it concerning military operations. This is due to its dominance in that arena and also because it crushed other movements within Gaza with an iron fist (not just Fatah-related groups but others, too). In the West Bank, Hamas continues to have both political and social organization and it has maintained significant operational capabilities there, although much less than in Gaza. Notably, there is not thought to be any rocket arsenal in the West Bank.

All this is to say is that Hamas is an entrenched, robust, multifaceted part of the Palestinian scene. It has many capabilities and partnerships and cannot be easily eliminated. The presence of Hamas's political leadership in Qatar has had the explicit approval of both the United States and Israel. Israel facilitated significant cash transfers from Qatar to the Hamas government. This implicit partnership between the Israeli government and Hamas may have been one reason for the reduced security presence on the ground.

While Hamas and Iran are very close, theirs is a very different relationship than that between Hezbollah and Iran. The Iranian Revolutionary Guard Corps (IRGC) set up Hezbollah. Hezbollah has kept Iranian Supreme Leader Ayatollah Khamenei as its spiritual guide (which itself caused a split with the late Lebanon-based Ayatollah Mohammed Hussain Fadlallah), and it is almost exclusively funded and armed by Iran. Hezbollah also shares the same Shiite ideology (both as Twelver Shiites and notions around Vilayet-i-Faqih).

Hamas originates much more from the Muslim Brotherhood movement and modern Sunni Islamism. Its association with Iran came later and out of convenience as it had to flee various Arab jurisdictions over time due to pressure from the United States. However, it has an autonomous political decision-making system. It is also driven by its own core ideology.

Ultimately, that means in this conflict, while Hamas is 'practical' as it governs Gaza, it sees its mandate as beyond Gaza and across all Palestinian territories and populations. Gaza is a means, not an end. While it has offered Israel many truces, it has never given up any territorial claims over the entirety of Israel itself (beyond the Palestinian territories). Furthermore, it is distinctly an Islamist organization that believes in Islamic supremacy. From its actions, including this recent set of attacks, it has characterized Jewish civilians, including within Israel, as settlers, and it is questionable how welcome they would ever be under hypothetical Hamas rule.

Given most Palestinians in Gaza are refugees or descendants of refugee populations from towns within modern-day Israel (inside the Green Line), many still seek to return to those same areas. The convergence of Hamas with Gaza means that it has likely hardened, not eased, its ideology. Any short-term truce or détente with Hamas only means that it will retrench for a more protracted battle.

All this being said, the idea that the Palestinian population is captive to Hamas is also a bit of a mischaracterization. Hamas is part of the fabric of the Palestinian population because there is no politically or militarily organized alternative in Gaza. Again, this has been due to a concerted effort by Israel since the death of Yasser Arafat; it occurred not by accident but in line with many publicly stated intentions. Given this reality, Hamas has wide latitude, given broader support in Gaza, unlike Hezbollah in Lebanon overall.

Financially, like Hezbollah, Hamas benefits from a constellation of companies and financing mechanisms in addition to state support, public support, and the funds brought from Qatar and Iran. Recently, it was asserted that crypto assets are part of this, but that is not fully clear (and, if true, to what extent).

Finally, Iran likely had a strong hand in helping Hamas to organize for the October 7 attacks, perhaps in providing technology that enabled communications jamming, for example. Hamas may have taken the lead in planning, may have led the attacks itself, and may have even developed some of the rocket technology, but Iran would have been part and parcel of some aspects of the planning, although perhaps not aware of all the details, timing, and scope of the planned attacks. In some ways, Iran could have seen the operation as 'revenge' for the assassination of Qasem Soleimani and a way to re-establish its deterrence capabilities.

It must be noted Hamas has existed in some form for nearly half a century. It does not start and stop in Tehran; it would be a mistake to see this conflict as just a proxy war with Iran.

### 5. How much is the crisis about Israel and Palestine versus the broader Arab world or the Middle East?

This is not 1948, nor 1973, nor even 2000. Today, Israel is no longer occupying parts of Egypt, Jordan, or Lebanon, as it once was. In Lebanon, a contested piece of land, Sheba'a Farms, is still under Israeli control; however, it is not even clear if that is Syrian or Lebanese territory. It is also unpopulated. In Syria, the Golan Heights continues to be held by Israel. While President Donald Trump's administration asserted the Golan is part of Israel (acquired by force in 1967), that claim has no international recognition. The Druze communities in the Golan have some equilibrium and have developed close links in both Syria and Israel.

Beyond its immediate surroundings, Israel had been expanding relationships formally with Bahrain, the United Arab Emirates, and Morocco, and informally with Saudi Arabia. Its relations with Turkey had also been at a strong point. Of course, and significantly, the rivalry with Iran remained. Yet, even in proxy environments, such as Iraq and Yemen, the (recent) focus for its rival Iran had been on de-escalation rather than activation of new fronts from which to threaten Israel.

While the Palestinian cause is popular in the Arab world—and in sentiment across the Muslim world—this issue has declined in recent years in terms of priority. The over-whelming majority of Arabs and Muslims still carried deep sympathy for the plight of Palestinians. Nevertheless, other issues of concern closer to home were the focus.

Prior to the October 7 attacks, nothing had recently been bubbling in the broader Middle East about Israel. If there was any dismay in political circles, it was that the Israeli government was somewhat dysfunctional and included extremist elements. And many countries, such as Egypt, felt that the long-term lack of a political process for the Palestinian issue was a critical risk.

Yet, the current conflict, while focused initially on Israel and Palestine, has high potential to spiral into a wider conflict, which very few want, including Iran. And while people may be frustrated, there is no group of millions of Arabs ready to get on planes and join a military invasion or defense of Palestine. Aside from solidarity and street protests, the weight of concern is limited in terms of action. This, again, could change dramatically if the conflict intensifies. And there is rising anger across several countries, including neighboring Egypt and Jordan.

This overall frame is partially due to exhaustion in the region. The last 15 years have seen conflict after conflict, revolutions followed by counter-revolutions, and the disintegration of entire states. This era witnessed the forever U.S. War on Terror, the metastasizing invasion of Iraq, and constant (emotionally, physically, and monetarily) draining flare-ups between Israel and Gaza on multiple occasions.

Nevertheless, the legacy of militant groups, existing ideologies, and contagion effects, which are all still there, may suddenly come to the fore and alter the dynamic of a localized conflict. This could then engulf the entire region in ways that cannot be imagined right now.

## 6. Has a similar conflict happened before? What transpired?

While Israel has been engaged in many conflicts, both state-to-state as well as asymmetric, over the years (as will be covered in the following chapters), it might be appropriate to compare this round of fighting to those with Hamas in recent years. Outside of flare-ups and intermittent exchanges (too innumerable to count), there have been three primary rounds of fighting:

- **First Gaza War (2008–2009)** – The war lasted about three weeks, with a significant ground invasion. While ferocious, resulting in over 1,000 Palestinian casualties and a dozen Israeli deaths, there was no immediate cause. A breakdown of a previous cease-fire negotiated by Egyptian authorities precipitated the fighting. Egypt mediated the end of the subsequent round of hostilities. There was limited real change on the ground. And

Gilad Shalit, a soldier captured in 2006, remained in Hamas's hands.

- **Second Gaza War (2014)** — Lasting over a month, this round of fighting resulted from skirmishes in the West Bank after several Israelis were kidnapped (and subsequently found dead). About 2,000 Palestinians were killed, along with 70 Israelis. There was a limited ground invasion that aimed to destroy the tunnel network. The conflict ended with few changes on the ground, and both sides claimed victory. Egypt again played a role in bringing about a détente.

- **Gaza clashes (2021)** — This limited conflict, at the beginning of the Biden administration, lasted for two weeks and led to roughly 250 Palestinian deaths and about a dozen on the Israeli side. In the two weeks, Israel conducted 1,500 air strikes and Hamas fired slightly fewer than 5,000 rockets. Both sides seemed to be testing each other after the Trump presidency. A cease-fire was reached with Qatar and Egypt mediating, and President Biden was also involved.

The intensity of the current conflict already outpaces what has happened previously. Firstly, in other conflicts Israel never faced, from either Hamas or Hezbollah, such an intrusive incursion territorially. A typical incursion would have been a cross-border raid with fewer than five casualties or several kidnapped soldiers. The number of Israelis dead is essentially equal to that of every single conflict and terror attack combined over the last two decades. The deaths from Israeli assault on Gaza have already surpassed 30,000. This, again, is more than all the Gaza clashes/conflicts combined, including the Second Intifada.

It should be clear that the violence of the situation is unprecedented. It also cannot be compared to the 2006 war with Hezbollah, which was precipitated by a limited cross-border raid. The death toll on both sides already far exceeds even that violent conflict. In addition, Egypt cannot even mediate the proper opening of the Rafah crossing. It has a more limited role this time around.

Strategically, the Israeli government had two principal objectives after October 7:

1) obtain the release of all hostages, and

2) re-establish deterrence capacity.

Given the breakdown of the implicit détente on October 7, the Israeli government will not trust a new deal with Hamas. It will seek to kill as much of the Hamas leadership within Gaza as possible. After that, it is unclear who would rule Gaza (which would lead to the problem of no one ruling Gaza).

As a result of this strategic ambiguity regarding Palestinian leadership in Gaza, there is no clear endgame for Israel. As for Hamas, it was likely desirous of a wider third intifada that also encompassed the West Bank and an overthrow of the Palestinian Authority. In view of the nature of the operation, it had to be seen as a point of no return to reshape the political map within the territories and precipitate a long-term war.

The example of the U.S. invasion of Afghanistan is probably the most instructive conflict. The Taliban were and still are ruthless. The United States removed the government, occupied Afghanistan, installed a new government, spent hundreds of billions of dollars, killed thousands of people, jailed thousands of Taliban rank-and-file, and decapitated the leadership, only to leave Afghanistan back in the hands of the Taliban.

Yes, it took 20 years, but that is a blink of an eye now in this conflict. It has already been 25 years since Israel tried to assassinate Hamas leader Khaled Meshaal in Amman, Jordan. The long game is still playing out.

## 7. How might all this unfold this time around?

### Gaza

Within the operational theater of Gaza, there have been expanding ground incursions through early 2024. The hope for the safe release of hostages has declined significantly with these ground incursions. Israel did not take particular heed to the extent of civilian casualties. For Israel, the models were Raqqa and Mosul—U.S. forces leveled those cities to the ground to retake them from ISIS—or maybe even Dresden in World War II. Some observers feel that what has happened in Gaza in the months after the October 7 attacks has already exceeded whatever the U.S. did against ISIS.

The assumption has to be that airstrikes will continue and ground incursions will intermittently continue throughout the entirety of Gaza. While the airstrikes have hit everywhere, the ground incursions have moved from one part of the Strip to another, almost clinically. The idea has been to level neighborhoods with airstrikes before moving in. During the first months of ground incursions, the rocket fire from Gaza did not abate. It thus is not clear how extensive the arsenal of Hamas is, but certainly, if the conflict continues through the end of 2024, it will be depleted.

By the end of this current round of conflict, Israel may see its highest number of casualties since the Yom Kippur War, around 2,500. This would be shocking for Israeli society. Thus far, it is not fully clear how many military casualties there have been, due to intermittent media restrictions in Israel. At this point, the Netanyahu government would consider it a defeat if Hamas is still ruling Gaza before a full cease-fire is established. Hamas was looking for hand-to-hand combat on the ground, and it appears it has been arguably as effective as Hezbollah was in 2006, especially as the war has dragged on.

### Palestinian territories and communities

Initially, there were growing clashes in the West Bank. The Israeli government also initially distributed weapons to settlers, who were carrying out attacks. The West Bank, however, did not see sustained conflict, even as the Gaza incursions intensified. There will continue to be sustained military activity in the West Bank by Israel, including low-level air attacks and a significant Israeli troop presence. It does not appear, however, that there is enough operational capability within the West Bank for Hamas to mount any meaningful attacks for a sustained period. What may yet unfold in the West Bank could still be violent, deadly, and perhaps prolonged.

This then raises the specter of clashes within East Jerusalem and rising tensions with Arab communities within Israel. There are ministers within the Netanyahu government who view the Arab presence in Jerusalem as an irritant and the Arab community in Israel itself as a fifth column. In addition to massive civil liberties violations, there could still be mass arrests. However, there may also be more incidents of lone wolf attacks (several have already occurred or been thwarted), some under Hamas's direction and others more randomized. Jerusalem is a powder keg and could see more civilian-led clashes in 2024. Likely, Hamas has also been planning 'surprises' in Jerusalem should there be a desire to escalate or retaliate.

### Neighboring countries

Since the beginning of the crisis, there have been near-daily clashes on the Lebanese border between Hezbollah and Israel. An escalation that involves rocket fire from Hezbollah into Israeli civilian towns on a sustained basis could always lead to an all-out air assault on Lebanon itself. This would then lead to significant engagement from Hezbollah and cross-border raids. That, itself, would lead to more proactive attacks by Israel on supply routes in Syria, something that has already started.

As the situation escalates, there could be consistent attacks by Iranian-allied Iraqi paramilitary forces on U.S. bases. The U.S. would have to respond more strongly in Iraq, hit allied forces of the government there, and call on the Iraqi government to make arrests of senior figures (which could lead to the fall of that government if it went ahead, which is doubtful). In some respects, this cycle in Iraq has already been underway since late 2023 in a limited way.

Iran has also sought an intensification of the situation in Yemen and encouraged Houthi-driven attacks. Houthi-linked militants have disrupted shipping routes and even seized a civilian vessel and its crew. This has led to broader American engagement in the Red Sea to counter attacks on civilian ships.

In a broader environment of escalation, militia groups linked to Al Qaeda and remnants of ISIS may seek to both take advantage of the chaos and demonstrate strength by hitting American/Arab government targets in Libya and Sinai in Egypt, for example. An attack in early January

2024 in Kerman, Iran, was also attributed to ISIS-linked groups.

There could be further attempts at lone wolf attacks in the West itself, seemingly homegrown and 'spontaneous,' but more likely due to activated extremist links that had been on the decline. This would lead to Western support for airstrikes on suspected terrorist sites throughout the Middle East, mainly involving the groups mentioned above.

Despite this assessment, the conflict still does not reach direct engagement with Iran. It does not involve strong U.S.-aligned countries in the conflict, Morocco, Egypt, and all the Gulf states, except for the possibility of limited terrorist attacks in their territories. The medium-term regional escalation would be a flashback to the 2012–2013 era of the Middle East. Tremendous destruction, heightened extremism, deterioration of broader Arab-Muslim-West relations, rising terrorist attack potential in Europe notably, and instability—yes, all are probable. It does not, however, point to an unknown and unprecedented multi-front war on Israel or with the West or a significant realignment on a war footing of the entire region.

Thus far, the United States, while supporting Israel militarily, economically, and diplomatically, has contained reprisal attacks further afield in the region. While the United States has made significant moves against Houthi forces, it has also tried to limit the scope of that engagement and has kept a back channel with the group. Still, there has been and will be a growing force posture and low-level skirmishes that will be downplayed.

The one caveat overall is that the chaos of war can lead to unintended consequences. Errant missiles can create counter-attacks and lead to engagement previously not thought possible from countries in the region. Every week, if not every day, the risk profile of potential expansion of the conflict will need to be evaluated and re-evaluated.

Given rising inequality, ubiquitous inflation, and flatlining governments, much of the world has been on edge. What could emerge or re-emerge through expanding war, broader volatility, and inflamed passions is best left to the deferred imagination.

## 8. Might this grow into a broader negotiation of the New World Order involving China and Russia?

There are a lot of differences between a decade ago and today. While the U.S. is re-engaging with familiar terrain and familiar enemies, and those enemies are re-coalescing, the entire frame is different. For example, the United Arab Emirates has a direct line into Israel. Iran and the Gulf are no longer at loggerheads. Hezbollah has far less political support. The Arab Spring, as the preeminent threat to existing regimes, has dissipated. The Assad-led government survived the Western-supported attempt to remove it from power.

The region is also on a much stronger footing than a decade ago, and there is much more coordination. It is easy to have a meeting of Qatari, Egyptian, Turkish, Iranian, Emirati, and Saudi foreign ministers together today. Israel would have to take notice if that group emerged united out of a summit.

The longer the open-ended nature of the current crisis continues, the more likely Russia and China will enter the fray to provide a countervailing perspective. Until now, and in the near future, they will keep in touch with all parties and strengthen the lines, informally and formally, with U.S. opponents, both state and non-state, in the region. China did facilitate the Iranian–Saudi rapprochement. It may seek to host a Middle East summit if this conflict extends deeper into 2024.

However, the main objective of Russia and China would be to embarrass the United States and distract it from its own neighborhoods. There is no reason for 'own goals' through rash interventions by the two countries. The die is already cast, and on its own, through in-built escalation, the United States would face increasing challenges without much movement from Russia and China.

This is much more about the Old World Order than the New World Order. It is about the U.S. re-demarcating lines of control between those within what it calls its rules-based order and those outside it, in this case, Gaza. If Gaza is seen as outside the order, and forces from Gaza undertake a cross-border raid, then that is the primary violation. Everything else is secondary. For the United States government, the attack was seen as an attack on its rules-based order. The humanitarian aspects are all secondary, including the underlying dynamics of the Palestinian–Israeli conflict itself. This is also how Ukraine and Gaza tie together, as discussed in President Biden's first Oval Office speech on the Israel–Gaza crisis on October 19, 2023.

## 9. How concerned should Americans and the West be overall?

Very concerned. This is a dangerous moment. The war in Ukraine means both Europe and the United States are already over-stretched politically, economically, and militarily. With high interest rates, the debt burden is only growing for all countries, including the United States.

Very soon, trade-offs will need to be made. Simply put, there is limited room for one more large-scale war, mind the potential of a third conflagration elsewhere (everything is possible).

Substantive initiatives to de-escalate the Ukraine or Gaza conflicts are few and far between. Therefore, expect the military overstretch to continue. Politically, the Global South is exhausted from being dragged along for conflicts. Limited support will be coming, and using political capital here means it will be lost elsewhere.

Yet, beyond economics and geopolitics, the main concern will be domestic. With the upcoming presidential election in 2024 in the United States, the West is already a confused powder keg. Left versus right. Democrat versus Republican. Populists versus the establishment. Activists versus nativists. Debates about the Israel–Palestine conflict have spilled over into the public square. It will continue to make many conversations volatile and upend preconceived alliances.

The more significant concern than all of this is resurgent terrorism. Yes, there will be hate crimes. They are already occurring. Terror attacks, however, may be about to rise. They could start in Europe, mostly lone wolf attacks, and then perhaps become more organized as tensions become inflamed, time passes, and groups like ISIS and Al Qaeda join the fray. In the United States, organized terror attacks are less likely. However, this would become a concern one year into the conflict. Then, all bets are off in terms of a cycle of reaction/counter-reaction.

The muscle memories of the Western security establishment and regional forces are strong. Everything could snap back on this front, and people could be dealing with a post-9/11-era redux when there are much larger domestic and global problems to confront.

## 10. Should the West invade Iran?

This would be the World War III scenario. It should be avoided at all costs. No country should attack Iran at this point, even with an errant missile, never mind an intentional invasion. It may seem unfair. After all, Iran has been funding and helping to arm Hamas. Indeed, it is the one country perhaps most responsible for the start of the current round of fighting. Yet, all non-direct measures should be taken.

Thus far, Iran has not, as a sovereign entity, entered into direct conflict with either Israel or the United States. Neither country has shown any desire to escalate to that level. Even confrontation with Hezbollah (thus far) is contained within a limited area. And the other escalation points all involve irregular forces confronting the United States. If Syria was a red line for Russia, Iran is a red line for China.

If there is any hint of invading Iran, run for the hills.

## 11. What about international law, a rules-based order, and the United Nations?

There is a lot to unpack about these topics, but suffice it to say that appeals to non-power-based frameworks or entities will not lead to results. There is no coherent approach to international law and no enforcing mechanism beyond the pageantry of the International Court of Justice, where a case was brought by South Africa. The United Nations itself, politically, is simply a coordinating body. It can effectively deliver aid and send strong messages describing where a preponderance of the international community sits on an issue, but that is about it.

While appeals from the UN can provide rhetorical fodder or moral standing, they do not lead to any change in outcomes. As a neutral body, the United Nations will be at the helm of all humanitarian activities. Bodies like the ICRC will be at the forefront of hostage negotiations and coordination. A final resolution, cease-fire, or framework to administer Gaza may also be passed through the UN Security Council (UNSC).

Aside from this, there is little need to pay heed to the terminology of international law, fortunately or unfortunately.

## 12. What are the implications for the global economy, business community, and other organizations?

After each crisis, of which there have been many in the last two decades, there have been dramatic shocks. The world has largely recovered following the pandemic, when self-imposed shutdowns led to an economic slowdown and disruption of supply chains. Stimulus initiatives did lead to inflation; that, however, has not undermined the functioning of the leading economies. Finally, the Ukraine war removed Russia from the business map for the West, but many corporations managed to reorient.

Broader global instability has created pressure on energy prices, and the Gaza crisis is no different. Yet, little has affected (so far) supply routes for energy nor depressed demand. While there is a 'New World Order' at least in the making, it is not here yet. China does not seem interested in using this moment to add even more economic challenges by reorienting supply chains or making any shock moves.

For the business community and other private organizations, three primary adaptive responses are recommended:

- Firstly, all developments should be monitored closely, particularly if working with or through affected areas. That means businesses with operations in Israel, Palestine, Lebanon, Iraq, Iran, Yemen, Egypt, and Jordan should be on notice. There will also be escalating tensions, which could be exploited to create security incidents in Gulf countries and more stable settings. Escalations will mean that European cities may see clashes where there are high migrant populations. More broadly, Western organizations operating in Muslim countries, such as Pakistan, Indonesia, Bangladesh, and Malaysia, will want to reassess any public engagement, campaigns, or visits in 2024.

- Secondly, politicization and polarization will worsen, and staying 'out of it' is better than getting yourself 'in it.' A lot of people are getting caught in the political crossfire. Businesses and organizations should keep messages simple, empathetic, and neutral. While there will be pressure to engage, doing so may not be worth it because it is easy to make a mistake. That said, supporting recrimination against personnel who make political statements could also backfire. Take a free speech standpoint except in truly abhorrent circumstances. The political winds will be going back and forth for a while.

- Finally, continue to invest in parallel circuitry of operations. Like others before, this event only points to furthering geopolitical shocks, and the reliability of a single global operating framework is deteriorating. Ideally, operations in one part of the world should not affect another. Where possible, keep coordination multi-regional and international, but ensure operations, activities, and business results can be led regionally and locally.

## 13. How should individuals react or act differently in their community or personal lives?

Everyone needs to assess what this moment means for them at a community and individual level. Overall, there is no requirement to stand on the moral sidelines. If a person sees this as a moral moment, then that person should take the appropriate stand. Yet, know that any public stand or pronouncement will have implications. Furthermore, if individuals are not well-versed in the issues of the conflict, they may find themselves amplifying false information and could face backlash.

The current moment is so politicized that each individual is tempted to enter each issue and declare a position. Most of the time, this aligns with perceived political tribes. Step back and take a breather before posting anything or engaging in arguments. That time may allow for the reassessment of a previously held view or give way to a more convincing expression of the same viewpoint.

There are innumerable ways to show solidarity to all those suffering, contribute to the humanitarian response, and call on all parties for de-escalation. This is a minimum way to engage, but again, the optimal form, manner, or engagement bias will be up to each person.

## 14. Is there anything else to know?

Assume everyone is being lied to by many people in many ways about many things.

Trust but verify.

# III

# THE MAP & PLAYERS

This overview of the 'map' and the major 'players' within each country or group may be helpful to provide depth behind the implications covered in the prior chapter.

## FIRST CIRCLE—THE PRIMARY FOCUS

### *Israel*

Israel is a country of about 10 million people. While a majority are Jewish, about 20% are Arabs, which includes Muslims, the minority religious group; the Druze; and Christians. Israel controls and administers the West Bank (which it calls Judea and Samaria) and East Jerusalem, which are considered occupied by the United Nations (based on UNSC Resolutions 242 and 338). The Israeli population includes the Jewish settler population in the West Bank, which now numbers over 500,000 and is growing. In East Jerusalem, the Arab population, except for limited exceptions, does not have Israeli citizenship but can vote in municipal elections. Israel does not consider most of the Jewish population in East Jerusalem as settlers, although the United Nations does; that population is also growing.

Jerusalem and Tel Aviv are Israel's two major cities, in terms of citizen population. Other major urban centers include Haifa (a mixed city of Arabs and Jews), Rishon LeZion, Petah Tikva, Ashdod, Netanya, Bnei Brak, and Beersheba. It is also worth mentioning Ashkelon, another major city in the South District next to the Gaza Strip, and thus, like Ashdod, can be more easily targeted by rockets from Hamas. There are many kibbutzim, essentially start-up towns (although many are now long-standing), including along the border with Gaza.

The political scene in Israel has always been volatile, and it is common for new parties to form and others to disband, for elections to be held all too frequently, for street protests to take place, for intra-Jewish confrontations and disagreements (either ethnically or religiously based) to occur, and so forth. There has traditionally been a strong judiciary, which became the latest bone of contention between the government and the opposition in early 2023.

The military and intelligence services are well-respected (although their reputations can suffer due to what would be seen as external failings in past conflicts). The Israeli Defense Forces (IDF) have three branches (air, navy, ground), with an intelligence organization (Aman). The Mossad conducts mostly external intelligence, and the Shin Bet focuses on internal threats.

There is much more to be said about Israel, its economy, and its technology scene, but other forums are better served to expand on this.

- **Benjamin Netanyahu** — The longtime on-and-off-again prime minister and leader of the Likud Party, he first came to power in 1996 when he beat Shimon Peres in the elections shortly after then–Prime Minister

Yitzhak Rabin's assassination. He was the prime minister of Israel during a spate of deadly suicide attacks by Hamas in Israeli cities. He is deeply polarizing but is also a survivor. Before returning in late December 2022, he was prime minister for 12 years (from 2009 to 2021). He expanded his cabinet to form a unity government at the beginning of the current crisis.

- **Isaac Herzog** – The president of Israel was a former Knesset member and leader of the left Labor Party. His father was also president. Herzog is considered a moderate in the Israeli context and sought to facilitate a transition from the Netanyahu era but did not succeed.

- **Yair Lapid** – The effective leader of the opposition has refused to join the emergency unity government currently under Netanyahu. He is the head of the centrist Yesh Atid party. He was a journalist, actor, songwriter, and prominent media figure before founding the party he now heads. He formed a coalition government with a range of parties who essentially all disliked each other (objectively). Still, they were in power briefly in 2021-2022, and he even more briefly served as prime minister.

- **Naftali Bennett** – He founded the New Right party and joined Lapid's prior efforts to form a coalition government, becoming prime minister for one year. Bennett has been on the political scene for a while and attempted to attack Likud from the right. He has an ultra-orthodox background and was also a software entrepreneur earlier in life. He remains influential.

- **Benny Gantz** – The former chief of general staff for the IDF for many years, he later entered politics, founding a new party and then a political alliance called Blue and White. He became defense minister (and alternate prime minister) in multiple governments over the past several years but was most recently in the opposition before the recent attacks. He has since joined the unity government as a minister without portfolio and is a member of the War Cabinet alongside the prime minister and defense minister.

- **Yoav Gallant** — The current defense minister and member of the Likud party, he had a solid military career but faced controversy that ended it. He has political weight but his influence in Likud may be limited and he has often clashed with Netanyahu.

- **Avigdor Lieberman** — Formerly the most controversial Israeli government official for his harsh public statements about Palestinians, he has served in multiple Israeli governments with all types of ministerial roles. He leads Yisrael Beiteinu, which he established because he found Prime Minister Netanyahu willing to make too many compromises during the Oslo Accords era. The party represents primarily a secular-nationalist perspective. He has so far refused to join the unity government.

- **Yariv Levin** — The minister of justice in the current government, Levin has driven efforts to reform the Supreme Court that precipitated one of Israel's most significant political crisis since its founding. He is a core ally of Netanyahu and a member of Likud.

- **Itamar Ben-Gvir** — A coalition partner of Netanyahu's government, he leads the Otzma Yehudit party. He is a settler from the West Bank and is accused of being a supporter of Kahanism. Many of his statements have been labeled as calling for genocide and ethnic cleansing. He is the minister of national security.

- **Mansour Abbas** — Leader of *Ra'am* (the United Arab List), an Arab Islamic party, he joined the governing coalition under Lapid and Bennett, which was a first for an Arab political party in Israel.

- **Ayman Odeh** — He heads the left political party, *Hadash*, and formerly led the Joint List, the traditional coalition of Arab parties in the Knesset. Odeh and Ahmed Tibi are two of the more established leaders of Arab communities in Israel.

- **David Barnea** — The current director of Mossad, he succeeded Yossi Cohen. Not much is known about his politics. He has traveled to Qatar since October 7, 2023 to focus on hostage negotiations.

- **Herzi Halevi** — The current chief of general staff of the IDF, he has ordered an internal probe into the October 7 attacks. An experienced military official, Halevi has been involved in almost all Israeli conflict operations since the 1980s, including both Intifadas and the previous rounds of fighting with Hamas. During the volatile politics in Israel in 2023, he tried to remain apolitical.

- **Yossi Cohen** — The former director of Mossad, he is as much a diplomat as a spymaster. He presided over the greatest expansion of diplomatic relations in Israel's history, particularly in the Arab world. He has had numerous business interests since retiring from service, including in the Gulf.

- **Shlomo Ne'eman** — The head of the Yesha Council, the umbrella organization of all Jewish settlements in the West Bank, he is seen as close to Itamar Ben-Gvir.

- **Yitzhak Amit** — By precedent, he should be the next president of the Israeli Supreme Court. Amit may be blocked, and this is important because this is part of the underlying political fight for the future of Israel that the current conflict has displaced as a focus.

## Palestine

The State of Palestine does not have formal effect in the modern state system. Historically, the British Mandate of Palestine existed for three decades before the establishment of the State of Israel. The Palestinian territories encompass the West Bank, Gaza Strip, and, as stipulated by the United Nations but disputed by Israel, East Jerusalem (an entire chapter can be written about Jerusalem). Overall, this area is called Palestine and is recognized as the State of Palestine by over 130 countries. However, it is not formally a member of the United Nations (it has observer status in the General Assembly).

The Palestinian Authority acts as the ruling body that nominally administers parts of the West Bank and Gaza Strip. The PA once had an office in East Jerusalem, but it was closed by Israel. In some ways, the PA is the successor entity to the Palestine Liberation Organization, which represents Palestinians globally, most of whom were refugees in neighboring Arab countries. Yasser Arafat helmed the PLO for three decades, and its headquarters moved from Jordan to Lebanon to Tunisia, then finally to Palestine itself.

Today, the PA and the PLO are headed by the same leader. While the PLO still ostensibly represents various global Palestinian interests (such as Palestinian refugees in Lebanon), it is now defunct for all intents and purposes. Similarly, it has a legislative body called the Palestinian National Council, which meets but, in reality, does nothing.

The PA, which is the entity that administers Palestinian territories, has government bodies and ministers and receives funding from a range of partners (including the United States). It acts as the representative of the Palestinians. The organizational setup appears straightforward because the PLO and PA share a common leader in Mahmoud Abbas. Should that change, it could present a thorny issue as many representatives of Palestine abroad are representatives of the PLO and not the PA.

Another complicating factor is the fact that Hamas effectively controls the Gaza Strip, an outcome of the Palestinian civil war in 2007. In addition, there have been no presidential or parliamentary elections (the PA's legislative body is the Palestine Legislative Council) for over 15 years. Fatah is the dominant faction in the PA. Interestingly, the PA maintains around 40,000 personnel on the payroll in Gaza, even though some do not work. This is to maintain their support for Fatah.

While predominantly Western donors support the PA, Hamas received significant financial support from Qatar to administer the Gaza Strip (but strictly controlled for humanitarian services or civil service salaries), with the tacit approval of Israel (to lessen any burden that would fall on them) and the United States. In addition, the linkages between Israel and the Palestinian territories are inextricable to both economies. A significant share of the PA's core funding consists of tax revenues that are in fact collected and held by Israel.

Approximately 500,000 settlers live in the West Bank proper. That means the legacy of the Oslo Accords still splits the West Bank into zones where the Israelis have complete administrative control, where there is shared control, or where the PA has control. There is heavy security coordination between the PA and Israel. There is also a Settler Council (Yesha) that can complicate matters on governance, security, and access.

Similarly, Palestinians in East Jerusalem who do not have Israeli citizenship often work in Ramallah, for example. Even in Gaza, thousands obtain work permits for Israel itself. The Israeli *shekel* is the currency used in the Palestinian territories. Israel still has relatively complete control over borders, the sea, and air (it destroyed the Palestinian airport in Gaza during the Second Intifada). The Rafah border is international, but Egypt has been hesitant to make it too functional as it has its own challenges in the Sinai, and Israel has strict requirements for entry and exit.

It gets even more complicated (of course). There are militant factions that are under neither Hamas nor Fatah. This notably includes Palestinian Islamic Jihad, which, in some ways, is more violent than Hamas. They also receive backing from Iran. The Popular Front for the Liberation of Palestine (PFLP) and the Democratic Front for the Liberation of Palestine (DFLP) are now relatively defunct and represent echoes of the socialist era of the PLO. Finally, the Al Aqsa Martyrs Brigades are a proscribed but still active militant wing of Fatah, which agitates violence in the West Bank primarily.

There are approximately five million Palestinians in the West Bank and Gaza. While traditionally Christians made up significant numbers, today they represent only 1% of the population. Prominent population centers, Ramallah (the administrative capital), and Bethlehem are traditionally Christian cities. Other urban centers of note in the West Bank include Nablus, Jenin, and Hebron. The latter city is a complete mess, spliced as it is due to Israeli settlers. In Gaza, the major city is Gaza City, and other significant municipalities include Khan Younis, Jabalia, and Rafah.

It is important to note that many Palestinians in these jurisdictions are refugees or double refugees. Many still actively desire to return to their familial hometowns in what is today Israel proper. In both the West Bank and Gaza Strip, the UN Agency for Palestinians (UNRWA) still runs schools for many Palestinians, a legacy of its role from the 1950s.

- **Mahmoud Abbas** – The president of the Palestinian Authority since 2005 and the head of the PLO. He was a close confidant to Yasser Arafat and succeeded him when he died. He is rumored to have had close ties to the KGB during the Soviet era. He is almost 90 years old.

- **Mohammad Shtayyeh** – A long-standing partner of Abbas, he serves as the prime minister of Palestine. Ultimately, he is not considered politically influential, but that might be said for many officials in Fatah.

- **Riyad Al Maliki** – The current foreign minister, he was once involved in more militant activities but shifted to democracy and civil society development. Again, like Shtayyeh, there does not appear to be much independence in mandate or support beyond Abbas.

- **Husam Zomlot** – Born in Gaza, Zomlot has emerged as one of the more effective spokespersons for Palestine, currently serving as the ambassador to the United Kingdom. He was the ambassador to the United States before Trump closed the PLO Mission.

- **Khaled Meshaal** – A long-standing leader of Hamas and founder of the political bureau, he still ostensibly directs Hamas from behind the scenes, even though he has given up day-to-day leadership. He resides in Doha and prominently escaped assassination by the Mossad in 1997 in Jordan.

- **Ismail Haniyah** – The current political leader of Hamas, he also resides in Doha. He served as prime minister after Hamas won the elections in 2006. In mid-2007, there was a split in the PA, and he effectively became the head of the Gaza Strip only. He moved to Doha in 2017 after becoming the overall political leader of Hamas.

- **Mohammed Deif** – Military commander of Hamas, he announced the Al Aqsa Flood operation in a prerecorded tape released the morning of October 7. He is a military leader within Hamas, who was also behind many of the suicide bomb campaigns of the 1990s. His wife and children were killed by an Israeli assassination attempt a decade ago.

- **Abu Obaida** – An established voice for Hamas going back over 15 years, his real name is not known (although the Israelis claim they have uncovered it). He often makes key announcements for the militant arm of the group.

- **Yahya Sinwar** – Effectively the head of government in Gaza, he leads Hamas's overall presence on the ground. He is a top target for assassination during the current Israel offensive.

- **Ziyad Al Nakhalah** – The leader of Palestinian Islamic Jihad, he resides outside of Gaza. He has very close relations with Iran.

- **Mustafa Barghouti** – A leader of a relatively independent political movement in the Palestinian territories, he placed second in the last Palestinian presidential election in 2005. More a civil society activist and medical professional than a politician, he serves as an informal spokesperson on the global stage. He is based in the West Bank.

- **Marwan Barghouti** – If there were a true successor to Yasser Arafat who could have maintained unity in Palestinian circles, it would have been Marwan Barghouti. He has been sitting in an Israeli prison since 2002. He has traditionally been a member of Fatah but has also engaged in military activities through the off-shoot movement Tanzim. He would be a leading candidate were he on a Palestinian presidential election ballot today.

- **Mohammed Dahlan** – The former strongman of the Palestinian Authority, he is waiting in the wings in Abu Dhabi for the day after. He is despised in Hamas circles and not necessarily popular elsewhere, but he may still emerge as a leader in future scenarios.

## SECOND CIRCLE—THE NEIGHBORS

### Lebanon

Lebanon is a country of 5.5 million people, with far more Lebanese outside Lebanon as emigrants. Home to myriad factions and sects, it was traditionally home to many fleeing minorities in the region (numbering 18 at an official level). Its capital city is Beirut, which reflects the variety of the country's character, culturally, religiously, and politically. Other prominent cities include Tripoli in the North, Saida in the South, and Baalbek in the East.

Syria traditionally claimed purview over Lebanon and has heavily influenced the country since its independence in 1943. The Syrian claim is relevant because its interference in the country only ended in 2005 after a massive political movement spliced the country into two rival factions (March 8 and March 14). Ostensibly, since then, Syria has withdrawn, but a related party, Hezbollah, has continued to undermine national sovereignty in the country by effectively controlling large parts of territory (with support from Iran).

Until 2000, this was somewhat popular (although, of course, not for all parties) because Hezbollah was fighting the Israeli presence in the South, which had been in place since the 1982 invasion led by Israel to dislodge the PLO presence. However, since the war with Israel in 2006, in which massive destruction and death was inflicted on Lebanon, Hezbollah has faced increasing political scrutiny.

After Hezbollah clearly and directly allied with the Assad government following the Syrian uprising in 2011, it lost considerably more support from within the Sunni population and came to be viewed as representing only a narrow set of sectarian and foreign interests. Lebanon remains caught between a web of political factions in place since the 1975 civil war, although with varying alliances. These most prominently represent the Christian, Shiite, Sunni, and Druze communities.

Most of the communities have multiple political factions representing them on a national level: Christian (Free Patriotic Movement, Kataeb, Lebanese Forces), Sunni (Mustaqbal, independents), Shiite (Hezbollah, Amal), and Druze (Progressive Socialist, Lebanese Democratic Party). There is a final civil society grouping that does not hold much sway, unfortunately, in parliament.

The Palestinian issue remains a concern because of the history of the PLO presence that came to Lebanon following events known as Black September in Jordan. The PLO played a big part in the civil war, primarily in the war's Muslim-left alliance. The Israeli invasion in 1982 led to the displacement of the PLO to Tunisia.

In Lebanon, however, the issue of *tawteen* has meant that half a million Palestinian refugees do not have official citizenship, as that would rebalance the national sectarian equation, given that Palestinians are predominantly Muslim. That means Palestinian refugees are cloistered in 12 refugee camps, where militant groups also organize (and could seek to engage Israel from along the Lebanese border). Despite the departure of the PLO, the overall refugee population has meant the Palestinian issue still has a significant base in Lebanon. The convergence with Hezbollah of many of the militant groups means that Lebanon is never more than one step removed from the Palestinian–Israeli conflict.

Finally, since 2000, there has been no real raison d'être for conflict with Israel; Hezbollah claims that the Sheba'a Farms are still occupied and uses this as a pretext for some of its activities. It also maintains an active armed presence in the South. Border skirmishes with Israel are rare, but there is intermittent violence, although nothing like in 2006. This is the real danger, and it is thought that Hezbollah's military capabilities are much more robust today even though it is much less popular.

Again, there is more to be written about Lebanon, such as its economy, inflation, and overall dynamics, that cannot be covered here.

- **Hassan Nasrallah** — Hezbollah's effective leader and secretary-general since 1992 (although it is unclear how decisions are made within the group), he is a charismatic spokesperson and a key figure in the Arab world. While he used to be one of the most popular figures in the region, that is no longer the case.

- **Naim Qassem** — The deputy secretary-general of Hezbollah is perhaps more of a figurehead than a significant decision-maker. It is unclear who is militarily leading Hezbollah today. After the killing of Imad Mughniyeh in 2008 and then Mustafa Badredinne during the Syrian war, this is an open question. It was announced that this figure was Mustafa Mughniyeh (son of Imad), but that may have been just for public consumption.

- **Gebran Bassil** – The son-in-law of the past President Michel Aoun, he is the leader of the Christian party the Free Patriotic Movement. Lebanon currently has no president, leaving some power in Bassil's hands. He has had a less cordial relationship with Hezbollah than Aoun. He is widely considered to be extremely corrupt.

- **Najib Mikati** – The current caretaker prime minister of Lebanon and an old hand in Lebanon's politics and business, Mikati is from Tripoli and has limited political support (in terms of a party base). He has been PM twice before, and in many ways is a default in the absence of a strong voice within the Sunni Lebanese community (the PM is traditionally Sunni while the president is Christian).

- **Saad Hariri** – The son of assassinated Prime Minister Rafiq Al Hariri, he is the leader of the Future Movement and himself a former prime minister of Lebanon. He has kept very close relations with Saudi Arabia but had a very public dust-up with the current Crown Prince of that country. While out of politics and dealing with eccentric legal issues, he is still the most prolific politician in the Sunni community.

- **Samir Gaegea** – The leader of the Lebanese Forces, a Christian party, he is a prominent critic of both Syria and Hezbollah and was jailed following the Syrian occupation of Lebanon. He also fought many militia battles during the civil war. His wife helped secure his release from prison during the political sea change in Lebanon in 2005.

- **Walid Jumblatt** – The most prominent Druze leader in the country, he is also the weathervane of political winds. His father led the Muslim-Left-Arabist side of the Lebanese civil war and was allegedly assassinated by then–Syrian President Hafez Al Assad. He has been a leader of the Progressive Socialist Party, although he has ostensibly passed on his portfolio to his son Taymour. His historical nemeses, the Arslans, who allied with Hezbollah, have been significantly weakened. Jumblatt remains a critic of both Hezbollah and Israel.

## Egypt

Egypt has the largest population in the Arab world, which seems to grow by 10 million every few years. It is likely around 120 million now, and greater Cairo teems with 20–30 million inhabitants. Egypt's second city, Alexandria, is on the Mediterranean coast. The country has the second-longest border with Israel after Jordan. Following the 1948 War, Egypt occupied and took control of the Gaza Strip, which borders its territory. This was lost in the 1967 war with Israel, which subsequently took control of both the Gaza Strip and West Bank, as well as East Jerusalem and the Egyptian territory of Sinai.

In 1978, through mediation by President Jimmy Carter, Egyptian President Anwar Sadat visited Israel and signed a peace treaty, demarcating the border officially, returning the Sinai to Egypt, and ceding any future territorial claims. This led to full diplomatic relations, although there have often been challenges in the relationship.

Sadat himself was assassinated in 1981 by militants opposed to the normalization of relations.

Groups closely affiliated with the Muslim Brotherhood led several attacks inside Egypt in the 1980s, as did other terrorist groups, including those led and supported by Al Qaeda's co-founder, Ayman Al Zawahiri. Islamic militancy continued to grow thereafter, including notably in the 21st century, in the Sinai, near the border with Gaza. That has created a key security concern for Egypt, as links between militants in Gaza and the Sinai can be problematic.

Before the Arab Spring, Hamas itself crushed several Salafi-jihadist-linked groups in the Gaza Strip to establish its totalitarian control of the territory. In that sense, it was pseudo-aligned with the Egyptian government. Of course, Egypt has maintained strong relations with the PLO as well. Throughout each flare-up between Fatah and Hamas and between Hamas and Israel, Egyptian intelligence officials have played a key role in mediating détentes, truces, and exchanges of prisoners.

The temporary rise of the Muslim Brotherhood to power between 2011 and 2013 challenged the status quo and led to a deterioration of relations between Hamas and the security apparatus in Egypt. Other challenges arose because Hamas enjoyed strong ties with Qatar and Turkey, who had reduced relations with Egypt. However, security needs and border coordination have since prevailed.

In 2021, Egyptian officials again played a vital role in reducing tensions during the flare-up of conflict in Gaza. The Rafah border has been intermittently opened and closed, but this has been subject to varying security needs of the day of the Egyptians or Israelis. Egypt has worries about smuggling, refugees, and militant links.

Overall, while the Egyptian population remains very pro-Palestinian, there is zero political will in the establishment for any form of confrontation with Israel. Any writing on Egypt could cover an entire volume of books. This excerpt only outlines what is most relevant to the current round of the Israeli–Palestinian conflict.

- **Abdel Fattah el-Sisi** – The president of Egypt rose to power in 2014 after supporting a coup d'état a year earlier against then-President Mohamed Morsi of the Muslim Brotherhood. With a solid military background, Sisi has cultivated strong relations with Saudi Arabia and the United Arab Emirates. Now in power for over a decade, he is seen as a critical regional partner for the United States.

- **Sameh Shoukry** – Egypt's foreign minister for the last decade, he is an established diplomat. He is not seen to have a political agenda or independent base and serves primarily as a close emissary for Sisi.

- **Abbas Kamel** – The current intelligence chief of Egypt, he is critical to any engagement with Hamas and coordination on the Egyptian border crossing.

- **Naguib Sawiris** – One of the more prominent of Egypt's businessmen, he played a central political role in the transition of Hosni Mubarak. He had begun calling for his ouster before even the Arab Spring. He represents a valve into the leadership beyond the standard political establishment.

## Jordan

Many Israeli politicians have said that Palestine exists to the East of the Jordan River—meaning that Jordan itself is Palestine. This has sometimes been a deliberate strategy, especially in the early days of the conflict. Jordan itself has since 1948 been engaged in a complicated relationship with Israel, trying to stay mindful of Israel's aspirations and its own desire for territorial stability.

After 1948, Jordan captured the West Bank, governed the territory, and administered East Jerusalem and the Al Aqsa Mosque compound. This area was lost to Israel in 1967 and renounced in 1988, as Jordan entered into discussions for a long-term peace treaty. The country has maintained, through mutual agreement, religious supervision of the prominent Muslim and Christian religious sites in Jerusalem.

Over half of the 11 million or so Jordanians are of Palestinian origin, although given different refugee inflows, this proportion may have declined. Most Palestinians in the country are Jordanian citizens, although some still retain refugee status. Notably, there can be tensions and political jockeying between the traditional tribes in Jordan and Palestinian communities. The domestic situation was on edge during the Arab Spring, when Jordan saw some of the largest protests in the region.

This contemporary reality, as well as the contentious history of Palestinian groups in Jordan, means that any aspect of the Palestinian–Israeli conflict inflames tensions easily in Jordan. The monarchy takes a strong anti-Hamas position and pro-peace viewpoint. It is not considering (definitively) cutting relations with Israel, wants to maintain a robust border with the West Bank, and would be interested in any outcome that strengthens the Palestinian Authority.

Historically, the infamous Black September events in 1970, in some ways a civil war in Jordan, led to the expulsion of the PLO from the country. The attempted assassination of Hamas leader Khaled Meshaal in 1997 and the concurrent spate of Hamas suicide bombings also led to the ouster of a Hamas presence in Amman. Since then, many Fatah officials have maintained secondary or even primary residences in Jordan. However, there are limited political operations conducted from Jordan.

Jordan's links in Palestine are deep, but its leverage is thin. However, given it has the longest border with Israel, any broader destabilization could lead to serious risk to the governing authorities there.

- **Abdullah II bin Hussein** — Hailing from the Hejaz area of what is now Saudi Arabia, the Hashemite family was supported in Jordan by the British. They have subsequently built a strong multi-generational rule in the country, today led by King Abdullah since 1999. King Abdullah continues to enjoy strong support domestically, especially amidst the turmoil in the wider region (although this has not stopped intermittent dissatisfaction in times of economic malaise).

- **Rania Al Abdullah** — The marriage between King Abdullah II and Queen Rania was notable as she is of Palestinian origin. Like many first ladies in the region, Queen Rania's interests have primarily been in humanitarian affairs, and she leads several initiatives. At the same time, during politically precarious times, she either is limited in public view or brought forward (when Palestinian sentiment is inflamed).

- **Hussein bin Abdullah** — The Crown Prince has been more in the spotlight over the last several years. Named after his famous grandfather, King Hussein, Prince Hussein recently married a Saudi citizen. His presence has created a feeling of stability within Jordan.

- **Ahmed Hosni** — The head of Jordanian intelligence, he has been at the forefront of relationships with certain

Palestinian factions and coordinates on the Palestinian file with other intelligence chiefs of neighboring countries with Israel. His influence is more in the West Bank than Gaza, and should flare-ups emerge there, he would be more engaged.

- **Ayman Safadi** – One of two deputy prime ministers and the minister of foreign affairs, Safadi is at the forefront of diplomatic engagement on the Palestinian issue. He is more present on the Israel file than Prime Minister Bisher Al Khasawneh.

## Syria

Traditionally one of the stalwart countries of the region, since 2011 Syria has been a basket case, falling into the abyss akin to Libya. The failed revolution, subsequent crackdown, and then civil war severely destroyed the country. Despite a re-consolidation of power under President Assad, support from Russia and China, and a détente with much of the Arab world, Syria has failed to emerge with any force.

It has continued to be used as a base of operations for Iran, which has solidified its presence in the country and created a militant corridor from Iran through Iraq, Syria, and into Lebanon that underpins the so-called resistance axis. The airports in Syria have also been used to facilitate the travel of persons and goods in support of these relationships. Israel has had no hesitation in repeatedly bombing Syria, where it believes these links exist, including since the October 7 attacks.

In many ways, Syria is in a precarious position. It cannot cease relations with Iran and Russia without an alternative. It cannot seek a de-escalation with Israel given that the Golan Heights are still under Israeli control. It also is unable to maintain complete control over its border (as the drug trade has also shown). The United States maintains a presence in the North, where Turkey also bombs related Kurdish positions. There is also an American presence on the border between Jordan and Syria that has already emerged as a flashpoint in this crisis. Overall, it is a heavily convoluted situation.

Historically, Syria had one of the two largest armies facing off against Israel, and in 1973, it participated in the Yom Kippur War and the surprise attack alongside Egypt. Unlike Egypt, it never reached a peace deal with Israel. Then-President Hafez Al Assad had relationships with U.S. presidents going back to Nixon. Under President Bill Clinton, Syria and Israel were the closest they had ever been to reaching a peace deal, which was very close.

The Golan Heights has mostly Druze communities who still maintain close relations with Syria. There is no real military mobilization there, nor is there expected to be. Syria's role, if any, would be to act as a facilitator for whatever Iran wants to carry out. It has no discernable ability to play spoiler or mediator autonomously.

Overall, Syria, with its population of over 20 million people, faces lots of challenges, including returning refugees. Its two major cities, Damascus and Aleppo, have both seen airstrikes from Israel, particularly on its airports.

- **Bashar Al Assad** — The president inherited power from his father, Hafez Al Assad, and is an ophthalmologist. He previously had a close relationship with Hamas leadership before expelling them from Syria when they opposed his crackdown during the Syrian civil war. He has surprised most with his staying power. He was widely popular in 2006 in the Arab world, but today, he is one of the region's least popular leaders.

- **Asma Al Assad** – The charismatic wife of the president also holds British citizenship and wields a lot of soft power in the country. Most of the country's humanitarian initiatives also fall under her leadership.

- **Faisal Mekdad** – The foreign minister has been at the forefront of the public rapprochement with Gulf countries, notably in recent years. He has been leading public meetings with parties in the region on the next steps in the conflict from Syria's side.

- **Bashar Jaafari** – A strong hand in the diplomatic machinery of Damascus, Jaafari was previously the ambassador to the United Nations. He is now the ambassador to Russia, and if there were to be a larger meeting in Moscow on the conflict, Jaafari would help facilitate it.

- **Hussam Luka** – Not much is known about Syria's intelligence chief, unlike his predecessor, Ali Mamlouk, who was a long-serving regime apparatchik. However, he has had a strong presence in conversations throughout the region, including in the Gulf. There is a slight chance that Hamas's political leadership will return to Damascus if it is removed from Doha as an outcome of the conflict, and Luka would be part of this move. This would have to happen with Israel's tacit acceptance.

## THIRD CIRCLE—THE WIDER REGION

### Iran

Alongside Egypt and Turkey, Iran represents a civilizational giant in the region, with a population of 90 million. Its citizen population is triple that of Saudi Arabia across the water, although its economy is less than half that of its (former) rival. Outside of the capital Tehran, other major cities include Mashhad and Isfahan. Notable also is Ahvaz, which has a heavy Arab population, and Zahedan, which has a heavy Balochi population, and both are traditionally restive (including with support from external parties).

Iran has remained outside of American influence since the Islamic Revolution in 1979, and in that way its posture shifted and hardened against Israel, which has become its chief nemesis. Yet, its nationalist stance, including in the Persian Gulf, has existed since the time of the Shah. It has also maintained some strong alliances that predate the revolution, such as with Syria (with a slight pre-revolutionary dip) and Oman.

The Islamic regime sees Israel as an existential enemy that also provides a raison d'être of legitimacy for its rule. In the last several years, following the U.S. failure in Iraq and Afghanistan, the success of President Assad in Syria, the stalemating in Lebanon, and the re-emergence of Hamas, Iran has felt even more secure in its footing.

This has meant that even in the absence of a nuclear deal with the United States, it has been able to strengthen relations with its Gulf neighbors, notably Saudi Arabia and the UAE. Going into this latest crisis, it was in a stronger position regionally than it had been in years. Globally, of course, the flagging nuclear deal has been of concern. Yet high energy prices and thus a desire not to remove Iran from the energy table due to the Russian-Ukraine conflict have meant that Iran's economy has suffered less than it could have.

Militarily, Iran appears as strong as ever. It has not only been able to continue to support Hezbollah and Hamas but also has built a formidable force in the Houthis while concurrently creating an entire apparatus of paramilitaries in Iraq that will take decades to disentangle. Whether its more conventional weapons can challenge Israel remains to be seen. However, it is clear that the assassination of Qasem Soleimani, while a blow to prestige, did not slow down overall operational abilities.

Iran remains under the strict autocratic control of the Supreme Leader with the fig leaf of religious layering. In the overall apparatus, the Iranian Revolutionary Guard Corps is heavily influential, not just militarily but also economically, controlling many sectors of the economy and businesses. Any foreign policy issue is also viewed through a domestic lens. Iran leverages Palestine to mobilize support when sentiment is low and creates a war footing to crack down on dissent.

A more detailed analysis could delve into the minutiae of Tehran's intentions. At a fundamental level, any sustained conflict and disruption of Israel is seen as having a strong benefit to Iran on multiple levels. It also will bring significant U.S. force projection; the depletion of American resources is a further upside. Currently, Iran appears to feel it has enough deterrence capacity and will face no direct attacks. It is not looking for a direct confrontation with the United States or Israel (yet).

- **Ayatollah Ali Khamenei** — The second Supreme Leader of the Islamic Republic and in power since 1989, he served as the president under his predecessor and the founder of the Islamic Republic, Ayatollah Khomeini. A master political type, he had limited religious credentials when he came to power and clashed with Lebanon's and Iraq's leading Shiite clerics. He turns 85 years of age in 2024 but is still very much in charge.

- **Ebrahim Raisi** — As with most Iranian presidents, Raisi is an emissary for the Supreme Leader. He is a cleric and is seen as politically conservative. Given the

Supreme Leader's age, on a de facto basis, Raisi is very active in taking many meetings. In that way, and perhaps more than with previous presidents, he will start to consolidate more power.

- **Hossein Amir-Abdollahian** – Iran's foreign minister, he is an established diplomat who also had close relationships with both the Americans and Qasem Soleimani due to various files he has held over the last decades, including Iraq. Given this, and perhaps even more than his predecessor, he has developed strong relationships with sensitive actors such as Hezbollah. He is at the forefront of coordinating Iran's regional relationships during this crisis.

- **Hossein Salami** – The Commander of the IRGC, he has been vocal in his public statements. He made a fiery speech on the Al Aqsa Flood operation, pronouncing it as the end of Israel. Outside of rhetoric, it remains unclear how strong he is on an operational level.

- **Esmail Ghaani** – He is the successor to Soleimani in leading the IRGC's Al Quds Force, which specializes in the projection of proxy forces of Iran in the region. The jury had still been out on his capabilities; that will now be put to rest, given the Hamas operation. Once the dust settles, it would be hard for him not to be an Israeli assassination target.

- **Javad Zarif** – The former foreign minister, he still has many relationships globally. Should the tide turn, he could find himself back in the fray in some form. For now, he is solidly on the sidelines.

### Turkey

At the World Economic Forum in 2009, President Erdoğan had a famous dust-up with President Shimon Peres, just after the Gaza War that year. An Israeli raid against a humanitarian aid ship (albeit led by a Turkish organization, IHH, with links to Hamas) in 2010 essentially further damaged relations.

Turkey has had close relations with Israel since its inception. Alongside the Shah's Iran, the three countries provided much of the security architecture for the West in the wider region during the Cold War. The last decade has been a nadir in relations between Turkey and Israel, which happened to coincide with Netanyahu's long tenure as prime minister.

Of course, Turkey has many other concerns besides Israel, both economically and politically. A G20 country with 85 million people, Turkey, under Erdoğan's leadership, has grown significantly economically; it has also been adjacent to nearly every Middle East political crisis over the last two decades. In addition, Erdoğan's Islamic political leanings—and pan-Turkism—have meant he has tended to involve Turkey more in the Muslim world generally and with Islamic movements specifically.

Before 2011, Erdoğan, alongside his chief advisor, Ahmet Davutoğlu, focused on a zero-problems foreign policy. This meant maintaining good relations with as many actors as possible while much of the region, particularly Iraq, was convulsing, and there were rising sectarian tensions. With the advent of the Arab Spring, the change in the Israeli government, and an overall shift in Erdoğan's domestic posture, Turkey began to take sides and be more interventionist.

Squarely in this posture was a closer relationship with Hamas, a worse relationship with Israel, and support for Islamist movements in Syria and elsewhere that opposed existing regimes in the region. Erdoğan became particularly close to Egyptian President Morsi, and the latter's removal led to a sharp deterioration of relations between Turkey and Egypt. During the height of the Gulf crisis that tried to isolate Qatar, Turkey sent military forces to Doha. At one point, it seemed Turkey was fighting everyone externally, and in 2016, there was also a coup attempt internally.

Fast forward to the United Nations in September 2023, Erdoğan and Turkey appeared stronger than ever. Turkey was prioritizing improving regional relationships on all sides. There was even a landmark meeting with PM Netanyahu. This came on the heels of a Gulf trip, where Erdoğan and Crown Prince Mohammed bin Salman of Saudi Arabia drove around in a Turkish-made electric vehicle.

Turkey has also played a critical role in Ukraine. It has provided valuable drones to the Ukrainian side. It has also diplomatically facilitated key wheat exports. Throughout the Ukraine war, Erdoğan has maintained a strong channel with Putin.

This is not yesterday's Turkey. Erdoğan has a new flank of advisors with strong global and regional relationships; the country has become very strategically adept. Turkey itself may end up coming down very hard on Israel, beyond rhetoric even, and re-strengthen its relationship with Hamas; it will not be isolated globally or regionally if it does. It is a vital middle power for the United States in global power dynamics. Regionally, the Gulf and Turkey are now close, and the former will not side with Israel against the latter.

- **Recep Tayyip Erdoğan** – Leader of the Justice and Development (AK) party, President Erdoğan became popular as the mayor of Istanbul in the 1990s. He has

effectively led Turkey for 20 years, first as prime minister and most recently as president, after promulgat-
ing changes to the Turkish constitution. He remains by
far the most relevant political figure on the scene and
is more important than ever to the AK party. While
outwardly ideological, he rules from a nationalist and
practical lens. His family members, such as his son-in-
law, often hold positions of power.

- **Hakan Fidan** — A close confidant of Erdoğan, he is the
  foreign minister and former head of national intelligence. Fidan is notably half-Kurdish. He developed a
  good relationship with Qasem Soleimani in the mid-
  2010s. He was also instrumental in Turkey's post-coup
  stabilization. He is one of the most networked diplo-
  mats in the region.

- **Ibrahim Kalin** — The current director of the national
  intelligence agency in Turkey, he was Erdoğan's chief
  advisor for several years. In this role, he helped build
  the infrastructure for the presidential apparatus of
  Turkey today. He and Fidan have worked closely
  together, and many files may be split between them.

- **Ahmet Davutoğlu** — Once one of Turkey's future leaders, he is now a marginal figure. Yet, he still carries the
  Islamist mantle, and after the inception of the Hamas
  operation on October 7, he released a fiery video in
  support. If the situation takes a turn for the worse,
  look for him to try to attack Erdoğan from the Islamic
  right.

- **Devlet Bahçeli** — A key Erdoğan ally and leader of the
  nationalist MHP, Bahçeli has often staked out a position to the right of Erdoğan on issues ranging from
  Russia to Armenia. The secularist opposition CHP usu-
  ally responds so as not to be outflanked from a nation-

alist perspective by the MHP. Bahçeli has been highly vocal, encouraging more action on Gaza.

- **Fehmi Bülent Yıldırım** – He heads the Turkish NGO IHH, which has provided humanitarian aid globally and notably in Muslim countries. He called for a blockade against Israel. Famously, IHH launched the Gaza flotilla in 2010.

## Saudi Arabia

The place to be today in the region is Saudi Arabia. The country of 35 million people is the leading economy of the Middle East (rivaled only by Turkey). Led by the Al Saud family and with dynamic leadership for the first time in decades, the new Saudi Arabia is still calibrating its foreign policy. It began on a more interventionist path under the Crown Prince but has since settled into a more accommodationist stance as it focuses on domestic priorities. Overall, Saudi Arabia has also distanced itself from heavily Islamist groups, seeing them as potentially dangerous for domestic reasons as it secularizes part of the society.

Saudi Arabia views Palestine from a distance. It was, therefore, ready, perhaps reluctantly, to negotiate a broader Saudi–Israel normalization deal that is now delayed indefinitely. Yet, while Saudi Arabia may eschew politics for economics, it understands the soft power that comes from its Islamic leadership and strong regional role.

In many ways, the current crisis provides an opening for Saudi Arabia to rearticulate its foreign policy for the years ahead. It hosted an Organization of Islamic Cooperation (OIC) summit soon after the crisis began and held high-level meetings and conversations with Iranian leaders, including between the Crown Prince and the Iranian president. To what extent it seeks to get in the forefront or support others, such as Turkey and Egypt, in their efforts remains to be seen.

However, in the past, Saudi Arabia has had relationships with Hamas, and these were re-established after the détente with both Qatar and Iran. The region's move to broader instability is not a possibility that Saudi Arabia wants to entertain. It will do everything necessary to limit the contagion effect of the crisis. This would mostly mean pressuring and incentivizing Hamas but also creating a robust regional coalition, indicating to Israel that the region is united if there is wider escalation (if it gets to that point).

There is a chance that the 2002 Arab Peace Initiative is properly dusted off. Once the baseline for any future solution to the Arab–Israeli conflict, it was received derisively by Israel. However, it set the terms for a full settlement of the conflict and recognition of Israel by all Arab League countries.

- **Salman bin Abdulaziz Al Saud** — The 88-year-old monarch has now ruled Saudi Arabia for almost a decade and has served as the governor of Riyadh. King Salman has largely devolved power to his son but remains a strong presence within the Kingdom, Al Saud family, and regionally. His backing to any initiative would be critical.

- **Mohammed bin Salman Al Saud** — The de facto day-to-day leader in Saudi Arabia is the prime minister and crown prince. After some tumult, MBS, as he is known, has re-established himself on the global scene. In an increasingly volatile geopolitical order, he is now viewed as a pivotal ally to keep onboard for the West. This will be the same during this crisis.

- **Faisal bin Farhan Al Saud** — The foreign minister previously served in the private sector and at the Saudi Embassy in DC. He is a steady hand and has led some of the more notable files for Saudi Arabia over the last several years, including the rapprochement with Iran.

- **Yasir Al Rumayyan** — The governor of the Public Investment Fund, he is prolific in global private sector circles and is seen as the conduit to Saudi's sovereign wealth. He is likely in conversations with U.S.-based business leaders concerned about the crisis. He may be relevant to shaping some of the domestic willingness in the U.S. to a de-escalation posture by mobilizing support with influential private sector voices.

- **Reema bint Bandar Al Saud** — The ambassador to the United States, Princess Reema has quickly developed strong relationships in Washington. Overall, she is playing a substantial role in coordinating U.S. engagement. Her father was Prince Bandar bin Sultan, the spymaster and former diplomat.

### Qatar

No country has played a more quixotic role in the region than Qatar over the last quarter century. Since the previous emir's ascension, Qatar has been in the middle of everything and on the side of everyone. After a quick but severe dust-up in the mid-2010s with its neighbors in the Gulf—Saudi Arabia and the United Arab Emirates most notably—it has emerged relatively unscathed and in a stronger position.

In 2022, Qatar hosted the World Cup, and once again, despite severe European criticism around human rights, it avoided any dip in relations with the EU. Qatar has hosted a Taliban Office, has maintained relations with Hezbollah, has strategic communications with Iran, and had sent pallets of cash (literally) to Hamas. It has done all this while hosting Central Command in Doha and corresponding with the U.S. on any military deployment in the region.

Overall, while Qatar may at times overstep and may choose its own adventures, it mostly takes the authorization of the United States, including when it first opened the Hamas office in Doha. Furthermore, its activities in Gaza are closely coordinated with Israel. While Israel does not maintain a formal diplomatic presence in Qatar, Israel and Qatar have had robust diplomatic channels, formally and informally, since the mid-1990s.

It is unclear, however, how this may all change. The Netanyahu government's policy of creative engagement with Hamas clearly failed. Part of that framework was that Hamas leaders would be relatively safe from assassination, and Qatar would fund the day-to-day government. Israel was aware of this level of support, facilitating the movement of Qatari officials to Gaza.

What remains unclear is whether a change in policy will mean that the Hamas leaders are demanded to be extradited or the Hamas office is closed. In the end, Qatar will maintain its independent footing but will also closely coordinate with the United States on any policy decisions. In the immediate term, as a conduit to Hamas, Qatar will continue to be instrumental in all hostage negotiations until resolution.

- **Tamim bin Hamad Al Thani** — The emir came to power in 2013 when his father abdicated, around the same time as the Egypt coup d'état. Relatively young, he has been firmly in power for a decade and is shaping the country's direction. He has been at the forefront of restoring Qatar's standing in the Gulf and has strong relations in Washington, DC. He is well-respected by Qatari citizens.

- **Mohammed Abdurrahman Al Thani** — The experienced foreign minister, he was appointed prime minister in 2023. He is a close confidant of the emir and part of the group leading Qatar's direction after the World Cup. He also previously served as chairman of the Qatar Investment Authority. He has been involved in high-level shuttle diplomacy.

- **Abdullah bin Mohammed Al Khulaifi** — The head of state security is not as much a public figure as others. However, behind the scenes, given Qatar's many links, he is engaged in key security relationships.

- **Mohammed Al Emadi** — The head of the Qatari Committee for the Reconstruction of Gaza, he was the envoy to the Gaza Strip. He established critical relations with Israel and Hamas and would visit the Strip via Israel.

There are several others, such as ministers of state Lolwah Al Khater, Sultan Al Murakhi, and Mohammed bin Abdulaziz Al Khulaifi, who have played increasingly visible roles during the current crisis.

### United Arab Emirates

In recent years, the UAE has been less engaged on a direct level with the Israeli–Palestinian conflict. Yet, it also was at the center of the Abraham Accords, spearheaded by President Trump, for normalizing relations with Israel. During a multi-year lull in intense fighting, there was a rising feeling that the calm provided an opening for normalization. This also came during a period of complicated relations with Iran.

The Abraham Accords were celebrated in the West, derided in the Palestinian territories, and quietly accepted in the UAE. Most Gulf countries had already maintained close diplomatic and rising security relationships with Israel. Some of this was driven by Yossi Cohen, then director of the Mossad. Yet, the growing ties were also helped by several Israeli security businesses and other intermediaries in Washington, DC.

From a humanitarian perspective, the UAE has been a strident critic of Israel's actions. However, it has also viewed Hamas as representing two Islamist ideologies it considers existential threats—Iran's Islamism and the Muslim Brotherhood. In some ways, Hamas combines the worst of all worlds for Abu Dhabi's leadership.

This crisis may have played out in a particular way several years ago. At that time, however, President Trump was still in power, Iran was at loggerheads with the GCC, and the UAE was still at odds with Qatar. Times have changed in the region. Netanyahu also may have over-stayed his political welcome. Today, the UAE, much like Saudi Arabia and Turkey, is interested in less, not more, external problems, as it focuses on domestic priorities. Its overwhelming stance will be non-engagement and the containment of any escalation.

Should the crisis continue, the UAE may look to leverage its status as an Abraham Accord country, which it views as a long-term arrangement. However, Israel needs to be careful not to take this for granted. Overall, compared to other countries in the region, the UAE will take a very patient approach before any decisive moves.

- **Mohamed bin Zayed Al Nahyan** — The ruler of Abu Dhabi and the president of the UAE, he spent nearly two decades as Crown Prince, a position now held by his son Khalid bin Mohamed. He was previously quite engaged in managing defense and international portfolios for his father, Sheikh Zayed. MBZ, as he is known, is a pragmatist who looks at the long-term security architecture of the region, which he saw Israel as a part of. As the world changes, MBZ may also adjust the strategic approach the UAE is taking.

- **Mohammed bin Rashid Al Maktoum** – The ruler of Dubai, he is also the country's prime minister. MBR, as he is known, does not focus on UAE foreign policy. However, he directs significant humanitarian efforts from the UAE. In addition, Dubai has a sizeable Arab emigrant population, which includes Palestinians. Social and media mobilization from Dubai is swaying considerable attention globally to the crisis.

- **Abdullah bin Zayed Al Nahyan** – The foreign minister of the UAE, ABZ, as he is known, is the lead representative to international summits on the crisis. While an influential minister, he is unlikely to originate initiatives unless specifically directed by the president.

- **Tahnoon bin Zayed Al Nahyan** – The most enigmatic figure in the country, TBZ, as he is known, leads several sovereign wealth funds and a number of private companies and is the deputy ruler of Abu Dhabi. In addition, he has been engaged in security files as the national security advisor and was vital to restoring relations with Iran. If there were a UAE meeting with Khaled Meshaal, TBZ would lead it.

- **Anwar Gargash** – The visible 'spokesperson' of political files in the region for the UAE, he now serves as a presidential advisor on foreign affairs. He was the minister of state of foreign affairs for a long time, supporting Sheikh Abdullah. He remains a critical voice.

- **Reem Al Hashimy** — A minister of state, she is responsible for global humanitarian aid and leading policy engagement on several foreign affairs files. She may be a rising voice on aspects of a humanitarian cease-fire.

- **Yousef Al Otaiba** — The long-standing ambassador to the United States is effectively the dean of the diplomatic corps in Washington. Ambassador Otaiba has also been a long-serving international affairs advisor to MBZ, dating back three decades. He is extremely plugged into the think-tank, media, and advocacy scenes in the United States and is well-respected.

- **Lana Nusseibeh** — The UAE's ambassador to the United Nations is originally from the famous Jerusalemite Nusseibeh family. The experienced diplomat has represented the UAE for many years, including recently as she sat as the Arab representative on the Security Council. Nusseibeh will continue to play a critical role in various negotiations at the UN.

### Iraq

Iraq has been one of the stalwart countries in the region, like Syria. It sits at the crossroads of the Levant and the Gulf. In the 1970s, Iraq, driven by oil wealth and a stable government, including under the rule of Saddam Hussein, paced the Arab world regarding health and education standards.

The Iran–Iraq war, driven by rising hostility between the two countries following the Islamic Revolution in Iran, created an irreversible set of dynamics that has left Iraq in its ever-recovering situation of today. The sectarian strife that unfolded in the last three decades created significant regional linkages from and to Iraq for various Sunni and Shiite groups and movements.

Today, Iraq and Iran have a much closer relationship. Syria and Iraq, which had troubled relations for many years, also have strong avenues of cooperation today. And while the U.S. invasion has been much lamented and caused massive destruction, American bases still exist in the country. Meanwhile, the Gulf War is now a memory, and Iraq has rebuilt relations across the Gulf Cooperation Council (GCC) countries.

While ISIS was defeated, remnants of the group are thought to still exist in parts of Iraq and Syria. And their defeat came at the hands of popular militias, primarily formed under Iranian guidance. They have never disbanded. Although Iraq's government is focused on domestic priorities, sub-state groups could reassert their writ, which could push Iraq to the forefront of a wider conflagration with Israel. The large cache of conventional weapons within Iraq is also very much in the hands of the militias.

Greater entanglement of the U.S. in the region would most likely grow from tit-for-tat attacks between bases in Iraq and nearby militias. Given the many factions and groups in the country, it is hard to cover all the players on these pages.

- **Abdul Latif Rashid** – The president's election was assisted by past Prime Minister Nouri Al Maliki. He is Kurdish (as per custom) and is not a high-profile political figure. He has been in government since the early days of the U.S. invasion in 2003.

- **Mohammed Shia Al Sudani** – The prime minister was a member of the Dawa Party for many years before resigning that affiliation several years back. Since the election, he has sought to balance the views of both Iran and the United States. Yet, it is hard to ignore that

he is backed in parliament by proxy political representatives of some of the Iran-backed militias themselves.

- **Fuad Hussein** — The foreign minister is a Kurdish politician who has been close to Masoud Barzani. While
he does not have particular prominence, he has good
working relationships with the foreign ministers of
Iran, Russia, and Syria and the American secretary of
state. This raises the possibility of Hussein's role in
reducing tensions if needed.

- **Nouri Al Maliki** — The former prime minister was a
long-standing Saddam opponent, including in exile
in Iran and Syria. He was a leader of the Dawa Party,
and during his time as PM, the country descended into
chaos and war with the emergence of ISIS. He is viewed
as highly sectarian and close to Iran. Yet, he is also a
shrewd survivor, and today, from behind the curtain,
he may still be the most powerful politician in Iraq.

- **Muqtada Al Sadr** — The former populist 'hope' of Iraq,
he saw his political ambitions fade with the government that formed in 2022. Yet, he still holds tremendous sway and can mobilize the largest in-country
demonstrations. He comes from a family with a long
lineage of religious leadership.

- **Qais Al Khazali** — The leader of the Iran-backed Asa'ib
Ahl Al Haq group in Iraq, he is wanted by the United
States. He has met with Hamas leadership in Baghdad
in the past, and it is thought his militia is an integrated
part of the so-called resistance axis.

- **Ayatollah Ali Al Sistani** — The leading Shiite cleric
globally has been an instrumental but gentle voice in
Iraq at moments of inflection. He is less relevant today
due to age, but the organization underneath him is no
less influential due to its resources and reach.

## Yemen

Yemen is part of the historic fabric of the region and has been a civilizational crossroads. British intrigue followed Ottoman intrigue in the 20th century. Subsequently, amidst the anti-colonial and nationalist revolts of the region, the country became a battleground for monarchist and republican rivalries between regimes of the region in the 1960s.

The area had been home to many distinct religious and other groupings, particularly the Zaydi Shiite community. The last Zaydi *imamate* (kingdom) essentially ended in 1962 with the death of Ahmad bin Yahya. This gave way to a civil war and then two Yemeni states, in the North and South. Eventually, they unified (long story) and were led by strongman Ali Abdullah Saleh for decades.

Al Qaeda built a strong foothold in the country in the 2000s, and that defined U.S. engagement with the country for a decade. The Arab Spring in the 2010s led to a popular revolution, the overthrow of the long-standing government, and a civil war. In the civil war, the Houthis (or Ansarallah), who emerged principally from the Zaydi community, were the main belligerents. Gulf states, particularly Saudi Arabia, heavily intervened on the other side of the civil war, viewing the Houthis as Iranian proxies on their border.

Recently, while there have been broad peace talks, the Houthis continue to entrench their control in large parts of the country and effectively operate a proto-state. There is a revolutionary spirit in their movement, with large protests denouncing Israel taking place regularly in the capital, Sana'a. While the population of 35 million has been heavily divided, including religiously, confronting Israel represents a popular common denominator.

The Houthis wield a substantial arsenal of weapons and have formally declared war on Israel. Some of the long-range missiles that they possess and have already fired at Israel would need to travel over Saudi territory to reach Israel itself. There is a risk this could lead to renewed military engagement along the border with Saudi Arabia during attempts to intercept or obstruct missiles.

Pockets in the South and outlying areas in the East are controlled by militia groups allied with the administrative leadership council that international parties support. Saudi Arabia and the UAE have played a significant role in supporting non-Houthi forces in Yemen. Yemen's formal representative body, recognized by the international community, still omits the Houthis.

The U.S. has been driving peace talks, and there had been a considerable détente since 2022 in the country's civil war. All this is, of course, now under threat. Quixotically, since the October 7 attacks, it has been Saudi Arabia more than the United States that has tried to lessen tensions with the Houthis.

- **Abdul Malik Al Houthi** — The Houthi group's leader operates more like a Supreme Leader. While the Houthis do not control all territory, the majority of Yemenis live in areas under their rule. Al Houthi is relatively young and enigmatic.

- **Mohammed Abdul Salam** — The oft-spokesperson for the group also serves as a critical foreign emissary and negotiator. He has been seen in meetings with Hezbollah leadership and a range of regional representatives.

- **Rashad Al Alimi** — The titular president of the leadership council of Yemen, he is supported by the United States and several Gulf countries. He has limited autonomous power and has been in power since 2022. Previously, he served in the old Yemen government before its ouster during the Arab Spring.

- **Tareq Mohammed Abdullah Saleh** — A nephew of the late President Ali Abdullah Saleh, he sits on Yemen's leadership council. He has led militias in the conflict. Should Yemen be further engulfed in conflict, a proxy war could reignite against the Houthis. Saleh's family, in some ways, has the networks to take the most advantage and play a role.

## FOURTH CIRCLE—GLOBAL FORCES

### United States

While the conflict has started locally and has significant regional dimensions, it is also inextricably global due to the relationship between Israel and the United States. Since its inception with the support of President Harry Truman, Israel has been critical to the U.S. security architecture in the region, particularly in the Cold War. While significant people-to-people connections, cultural affinities, and other political interests are also at play, an underlying strategic dimension cannot be dismissed.

The layering of annual multi-billion-dollar security commitments going back half a century—which, unlike the aid to Egypt, also flows into research and development, joint weapons programs, and training exchanges—means that the security establishments in Israel and those of the United States are deeply interlinked. Whether due to this relationship or due to the nature of the world, the United States and Israel have faced many common threats over the last several decades, from Al Qaeda to Iran.

Nevertheless, the United States has had no vital national interest in maintaining the Israeli occupation of Palestinian territories and had distanced itself from labeling Hamas and Hezbollah as existential threats. Its specific interests in this crisis are apparent: maintain Israel's security (and deterrence), contain any escalation, and limit the reach of militant groups. Where possible, the United States will seek to prevent a rising humanitarian crisis as that would damage its standing.

The conflict is heavily precarious right now domestically for the U.S. If President Biden steps one way, he can be attacked as too dovish from the old right. If he steps the other way, he will be attacked as empowering war by the fractured left. Ahead of the 2024 election, there will likely be a forthright but waffling position that may lead to a vacuum of definitive U.S. leadership globally.

In the background, the United States is already embroiled in one conflict in Europe and is at specific divergence with global powers China and Russia. In past geopolitical flashpoints, such as when containing the nuclear programs of North Korea and Iran, China and Russia were part of the solutions framework. Confronting Hamas is purely a Western effort where the Global South has been unwilling to join.

From a political lens, the efforts are being driven from within the White House, with decision-making kept to a close circle. However, Congress has been vocal, and various Washington-led delegations will continue multiple trips to the region.

- **Joseph Biden** — The first-term president is a well-established Washington politician who has known Netanyahu for four decades and has a robust set of close relationships in Israel. His positions in support of Israel are no accident and align with his previous thinking; he will likely try to thread the needle as Clinton (unsuccessfully) did in the late 1990s.

- **Anthony Blinken** – The secretary of state has been alongside the president since his days in the Senate in the 2000s. He served in the Clinton and Obama administrations as well. Blinken is an old-school Democrat who may try to replicate a watered-down Oslo Accords approach in a new era.

- **Jake Sullivan** – The national security advisor was leading Saudi–Israel normalization efforts. He came into politics primarily via Hillary Clinton's campaign and was Biden's national security advisor when Biden was vice president. He remains close to Hilary Clinton; expect similar policies and outlooks on the conflict.

- **Samantha Power** – The former author and Harvard professor who built a career on warning against genocide, she became a White House official under President Obama and now leads USAID. While overseeing a large budget, she has been unable to provide any clear wins in the current crisis. Her absence is taken up by UN officials on the Rafah border, who have limited power behind them.

- **Lloyd Austin** – The secretary of defense was formerly a general in the US Army. He has also served on the board of weapons company Raytheon. He spent significant years in Iraq and Afghanistan during the aftermath of the War on Terror.

- **Barbara Leaf** – The experienced diplomat was formerly ambassador to the United Arab Emirates. Today, as the leading State Department official for the Middle East, the assistant secretary of state for Near Eastern affairs, Leaf is considered one of the valued assets for the administration in its regional outreach and approach.

- **Hady Amr** – The State Department's key envoy on Palestinian affairs, he was also the founding director of the former Brookings Doha Center. Behind the scenes, Amr should be expected to engage in shuttle diplomacy for Blinken with the Palestinian Authority.

- **Brett McGurk** – The lead coordinator for the Middle East on the National Security Council, McGurk is a survivor, having served the Bush, Obama, Trump, and Biden administrations. Some argue no other person can be as singularly responsible for U.S. foreign policy in the Middle East as Brett McGurk.

- **David Satterfield** – The special envoy for humanitarian issues in Gaza, he was recently brought back into the diplomatic fold in October. He is an accomplished ambassador with postings across the region. His appointment has not led to any significant results.

- **Charles Schumer** – The powerful Senate Minority Leader from New York, Schumer led a congressional delegation in October 2023 that had an audience with Chinese President Xi Jinping and then flew to Israel. Schumer represents the consensus view from the Senate and speaks regularly to the White House.

- **William Burns** – The current director of the CIA was previously the deputy secretary of state and president of the Carnegie Endowment for International Peace. He has also served as ambassador to Russia. During the Second Intifada, Burns held the same position held by Barbara Leaf today. Given his roles, he has experience negotiating with non-state actors and meeting with Hamas. He has been part of high-level negotiations hidden from public view, including with Iran.

- **Ben Cardin** – As chair of the Senate Foreign Relations Committee, he sets the high-level congressional agenda on the issue. He politically influences the White House's decision-making more than voices from the left in the House. Senator Cardin coordinates closely with others such as Senate leaders Schumer and Mitch McConnell.

- **Mike Johnson** — The Speaker of the House, he was elected in 2023, and comes from an evangelical Christian background in the Republican Party, which represents a key plank of support for right-aligned forces in Israel. Given the disagreement of views in his party on other issues, Johnson has rallied the Republican side around unity for support for Israel.

- **The Squad Plus (Ilhan Omar, Rashida Tlaib, Alexandria Ocasio-Cortez, Ayanna Pressley, and others)** — As the humanitarian crisis worsened in late 2023, the group re-emerged with ferocity. Ahead of the 2024 elections, keeping the base engaged will be carefully weighed against more centrist positions, which are aligned with Biden's instincts. How pragmatic the Squad can be will lead to more interactions or fewer with the White House.

- **Donald Trump** — Sitting on the sidelines of an issue that was his primary concern must be difficult for the vocal former president. Yet, the precariousness of the situation, his flagging relationship with Netanyahu, and the strong moves by Biden in support of Israel have put Trump on the relatively silent backfoot. Look for him to re-emerge, and when he does, it may shift U.S. debate on the issue, particularly in the Republican conference.

## Europe+

Here, Europe+ represents the European Union countries (27), partner countries (such as Norway and Switzerland),

and the United Kingdom. The EU has been relatively united except for some outlying statements by Belgium, Ireland and some Spanish ministers. Over time, however, the united front is shifting focus to a cease-fire and may descend to divided positions.

The conflict in Ukraine led to the most advanced security and political coordination between Europe and the United States since World War II. It also meant precise alignment of international messaging on issues of security. Officials like the European Commission's Ursula von der Leyen have leaned into this spirit. Overall, the calls from Europe to acknowledge the importance of Israel's security will always be balanced by calls for respecting international law.

Countries such as Norway, given the legacy of the Oslo Accords, also want to ensure there is always a peace process. Increasingly, though, Europe will be hard-pressed to deviate from the position of the White House in any meaningful way. Furthermore, domestic concerns mean that the policy approach may also be focused on terrorist disturbances, which seem to be a genuine rising concern.

As the crisis continues, outside of political support for Israel, humanitarian support for the Palestinians, and some back-channel diplomacy, there is a limited role for Europe to play.

- **Ursula von der Leyen** — As the president of the European Commission, she has recently become the most prominent pan-European leader on the global stage. Her profile increased during the Ukraine War, and von der Leyen has closely coordinated with the Biden White House. There are hints at divergence with the two European counterparts described next. She was a minister of defense in the Merkel government in Germany.

- **Josep Borrell** – The high representative for foreign affairs is a former president of the European Parliament and former Spanish minister of foreign affairs. He is close to the current president of the European Council and has a background in leftist politics. He has channeled the overall desire in Europe to drive a peace process rather than escalation.

- **Charles Michel** – The former prime minister of Belgium has the difficult job of aligning 27 countries towards one position as the president of the European Council. He has previously focused more on European rather than international issues.

- **Emmanuel Macron** – The President of France has the most robust relationships of any European leader in the Arab world. Notably, he is close to MBS and MBZ and has a good relationship with the Emir of Qatar. If the Gulf becomes critical to a solution, he will be someone to watch. Domestically, Macron must balance the volatile streets, which have seen competing protests. He is not due for re-election until 2027, so he may be able to take more political risks.

- **Rishi Sunak** – Untested by the polls, the British prime minister has staked ground on a heavily pro-Israeli position. Having worked in finance before entering politics, he has served as prime minister since October 2022. He will focus on shoring up domestic political positions in the short term.

- **Olaf Scholz** – The current chancellor of Germany is a seasoned politician and was elected in 2021. Leading the center-left Social Democratic Party, he has to balance Germany's historical sensitivities with its leadership alongside France of Europe. Ultimately, long-term escalation is not in Germany's foreign policy interest.

- **David Cameron** — The new UK foreign secretary, he famously presided as prime minister over the referendum that led to Brexit. During his leadership of Great Britain, he helped lead the anti-ISIS coalition and also led engagement with Israel during the 2014 Gaza War. He has many relationships in the Middle East, although Tony Blair still overshadows him and PM Sunak in the region.

- **Annalena Baerbock** — Germany's first female foreign minister, she joined the Greens early on and rose through the ranks to become the party leader. As the Greens joined the Social Democratic Party in a coalition, she was appointed to her current role under Scholz (she was also the Greens candidate in the election for chancellor). She has expressed strong support for Israel while also balancing calls to avoid a wider conflict.

Other European leaders may be less relevant to the region but may still seek to inject their perspectives into the situation.

### Russia

Historically, the Soviet Union had an in-depth series of relationships in the Middle East that, over time, represented a countervailing presence to the United States. In that respect, countries core to the U.S. security and energy architecture had limited relationships with Russia once it became an independent country after the dissolution of the USSR. In the 1990s, which was shortly after the war in Afghanistan, Russia's relationships in the Middle East were already quite dismal. With the two Chechen wars, they went from bad to worse.

It was only after the U.S. invasion of Iraq that the tide started to turn. Russia began to consolidate its domestic position and international capabilities at that time. In 2007, Vladimir Putin became the first Russian leader to visit Saudi Arabia. Further Russian engagement in the Syrian civil war in the 2010s projected its strength as a military power. Its sovereign wealth fund, the Russian Direct Investment Fund, helped build economic links. On the energy front, it joined a group labeled OPEC+, which allows it to coordinate energy prices with Saudi Arabia.

Throughout this time, Russia maintained strong relations with Iran, especially through nuclear cooperation. Through its links with Iran, especially in Syria, it developed an operations room with the participation of Hezbollah. There have also been high-level visits of Hamas to Russia. On the other side of the equation, Netanyahu and Israel sought and built high-level relations with Russia and Putin. This allowed for deconfliction in Syria when Israel had specific interests at play.

The Ukraine War temporarily slowed military cooperation and certain economic links between Russia and the Middle East due to U.S. sanctions. However, its presence, partnerships, and political relationships remain in-depth and multifaceted in the region. The Russians are very active and work primarily behind the scenes; many regional leaders have tacit respect for Putin. Since the Syrian civil war essentially ended, nearly the entire region has moved towards the Russian position on that file.

Russia sees Israel as a wedge issue for the United States. However, it still seeks to maintain a strong working relationship with Israel. Netanyahu himself spoke to Putin in the initial days after the October 7 attacks. While Russia may not be actively supporting Hamas, it continues to consult with Hezbollah, primarily through Iran, on various security aspects in the region. It also wants to contain any threat to Iran itself.

- **Vladimir Putin** — The president of Russia has been in power since 1999, either as prime minister or president. He is a consummate survivor and, in many ways, views the Middle East through the prism of U.S. intervention in Russia's own neighborhood. In that way, his focus areas in the Middle East are pushing back against U.S. encroachment on sovereignty, the survival of partner regimes, and opposing support for independence movements in friendly countries. Putin defers most files to his foreign minister and rarely enters high-stakes diplomacy. If anything, he is increasingly focusing on Ukraine while the U.S. is distracted.

- **Sergey Lavrov** — The long-serving foreign minister, he used to be the ambassador to the United Nations. Lavrov is nearly 74 years old and does not have the same agility to engage parties as he did at the height of the Syrian civil war. That said, given his role over the last decade, he can pick up the phone to anyone in the region, anytime, more than any other foreign affairs minister globally today.

- **Mikhail Bogdanov** — The deputy foreign minister is also over 70 years old; while he shares the crisis's diplomatic burden, age may also be a factor. He is the envoy of the president to the Middle East and has previously served as an ambassador to Israel. He coordinates with his Chinese counterpart, Zhai Jun, and leads dialogues with Hamas.

- **Vasily Nebenzya** — The current ambassador to the United Nations is a long-term diplomat. While not as active on the Middle East file, he is central to discussions around the several attempted UN Security Council resolutions by various parties.

- **Ramzan Kadyrov** — With the (dis)integration of the Wagner group, the president of Chechnya's forces remains the most deployable irregular contingent for Russia should the need arise, as it did in Syria. If there were to be a broader escalation, expect Putin to leverage a symbolic deployment of Kadyrov to the region. While this may be mere theater, it is still something to watch.

### China

China has increased its presence in the region over the last two decades. While it has been less active on a military front, it has been economically hyperactive. Today, China is the largest trading partner of Saudi Arabia and, overall, of the GCC. Much of this has been driven by energy trade, but non-oil trade is on a significant uptick as well. There are also substantial tie-ups in infrastructure, from telecommunications to petrochemicals to ports.

China is very present diplomatically throughout the Middle East and North Africa, and it looks to the region as a fulcrum of the Belt and Road Initiative. However, it continues to focus on economic relationships rather than intervening in various political files. Even though it may have opposed U.S. policy in Syria, Libya, and Iran, it has rarely interfered beyond diplomatic engagement, support for existing governments, or expanding economic investments. It has been decidedly less interventionist than Russia, even for its regional interests.

Its foray into facilitating the Saudi–Iranian rapprochement was, however, very intentional. It demonstrated how it could find spaces in a very American-dominant regional architecture to play a role not just on the fringes but on the main stage.

The idea of a Chinese-facilitated negotiation, perhaps through third parties, on any number of issues, including a détente with Iran, cannot be ruled out. In the current crisis, it would immediately focus on extracting concessions from Hamas, which it could achieve. China sees limited reason, however, to intervene as it has less at stake.

In the early 2000s, China had a growing set of defense links with Israel, which were essentially set aside due to American pressure. As such, it may feel free to pilot more aggressive postures targeting Israel. It would be difficult to see this rising beyond symbolism.

While China benefits from a Hamas–Israel conflagration, a broader escalation would be harmful to many of its interests. It would bring more, not less, American security engagement in areas where it is trying to deepen its involvement through American absence.

- **Xi Jinping** – As an individual, the president of China wields the most power in the world (Biden's presidential power is much more dispersed and transitory). President Xi's rise, background, philosophy, and governance principles are covered voluminously by other authors. In the Middle East, specifically, he has personally been engaged in building China's relationships in the region, particularly with Saudi Arabia. President Xi also met with Mahmoud Abbas in Beijing in the summer of 2023. In any long-term calculus, Xi views the Gulf as critical to China's interests, geographically, energy-wise, and in terms of transport infrastructure.

- **Wang Yi** – The once-again foreign minister, after a sensitive scandal involving his successor/predecessor, he has a long track record with the Middle East. He has continued to build strong relationships with Iran, Gulf countries, and Syria, most notably. He is an experienced diplomat and has a productive relationship with American Secretary of State Blinken.

- **Zhai Jun** – China's current lead envoy to the Middle East, he is the focal point for the country's shuttle diplomacy on the Gaza crisis. He speaks fluent Arabic and has served as a diplomat in several regional countries. In addition to political engagements, he is effectively China's media spokesperson on political issues in the region.

- **Zhang Jun** – China's ambassador to the UN, he is an experienced diplomat. He is at the forefront of coordinating with Russia's ambassador to the UN in offering alternatives to U.S.-presented resolutions at the Security Council.

- **[Opaque]** – Much about the machinery of China's engagement in the Middle East is unknown, much like the inner workings of China itself. The sudden disappearance of the previous foreign minister means that many do not fully understand the inner workings of decision-making in China beyond Xi's ruling philosophy.

### Global South
When it comes to the Israeli–Palestinian conflict, at some point, every country seeks to be engaged vocally and somehow play a role. However, a country's relevance may be minimal, either because it carries limited weight or because its engagement is not meant to expand beyond rhetoric.

Monitoring several countries or groupings is nevertheless essential as they provide critical bandwagoning support to any initiatives underway. Given interconnected geopolitical interests today, if the United States, for example, ignores too many voices in the G20, it could face challenges on other files, such as Ukraine and any new crises that emerge. This is particularly important in the Global South, an informal category that includes countries forming part of the Group of 77 (G77), and covers most of Latin America, the Middle East, Africa, and South and Southeast Asia.

- **Brazil** — With Lula da Silva's return to the presidency, Brazil is taking a vocal stance against escalation. If rebuffed by the United States, it could share in initiatives by the BRICS.

- **Latin America (outside Brazil)** — In Latin America, the Palestinian issue has been a regular cause célèbre on the left, and there is a broad diaspora, including many politicians who are originally Palestinian.

The current divisions caused by an inflamed global crisis could create new geopolitical dynamics. While Latin American leaders may have limited influence in the Middle East, they may seek to create a political mobilizing moment the longer the crisis goes on. For example, Chile, Colombia, and Bolivia were the first to downgrade relations with Israel globally. Argentina is moving in the opposite direction.

- **India** — Given its reluctance to join the international effort on Ukraine, the current conflict allows India to further position its policy independence from the United States as justifiable. India has strong historic relations with both Palestine and Israel.

- **South Africa** – With declining hard power, South Africa has sought to project its global soft power on the crisis, leading the case against Israel at the International Court of Justice. While symbolic, it demonstrates the increasing prominence of initiatives outside of the West on the crisis.

- **Ethiopia** – Ethiopia recently joined the BRICS, and the West has relatively ostracized it after the role of the government in internal civil conflict. Ethiopia has traditionally had deep ties with Israel, given the diaspora population of Ethiopian Jews.

  With the African Union (AU) headquarters in Addis Ababa, Ethiopia could still play a key role in bringing AU countries together on the conflict. There is a growing void across the continent, as seen by recent coups in West Africa. Behind the scenes, the conflict could be a wedge issue that China could leverage to facilitate political realignment on the continent.

- **Organization of Islamic Cooperation** – Broader dissatisfaction with economic conditions in populous Muslim countries, such as Bangladesh, Pakistan, and Indonesia, could spill over into anger toward Israel as a proxy issue. This, in turn, could prove a threat to existing governments. As a result, many unfolding implications within OIC countries must be tracked in real time.

## OUTSIDE THE CIRCLES

### United Nations

The United Nations is not an autonomous actor. It represents the proxy interests of the base common denominator of all global parties and cannot take any independent political stands. This is not a criticism but a reality of what the UN is and is not. There are several critical roles that the UN can, will, and should play as the crisis evolves.

Firstly, the UN is the lead neutral party to coordinate, deliver, and negotiate access to humanitarian aid. It has done this countless times in many conflict zones, including in recent years. It has navigated the terrain of numerous conflicts in the wider region, operating even in Taliban-led Afghanistan.

Secondly, the UN is critical to codifying agreements, particularly at the UN Security Council, and overseeing base-level implementation. This was the case, for example, with the implementation of Resolution 1701 to end the 2006 Lebanon War. Without this, achieving formal ways to conclude conflicts can be challenging. Thus far, only limited resolutions at the Security Council have been passed to advance humanitarian assistance, while various parties have vetoed other more substantive resolutions.

Thirdly, the UN can facilitate conversations that others cannot have. Israel can talk to Iran through a UN envoy, for example. Russia and the United States can communicate a clear position through the secretary-general. This becomes critical as the current conflict has many state and non-state actors in separate geopolitical realms in today's increasingly complex world.

- **Antonio Guterres** – The two-term secretary-general previously was the United Nations High Commissioner for Refugees (UNHCR). Before that, he was in Portuguese politics, rising to prime minister. He has presided over a tenuous tenure, given domestic turmoil in the United States and great power issues globally. Ultimately, while he has had limited achievements, he was considered particularly adept in the Syrian refugee response while at UNHCR. This could still be a moment he steps up as secretary-general. His invocation of Article 99 of the UN Charter in December 2023 was a move in this direction.

- **Philippe Lazzarini** — The commissioner-general of the UN agency—UNRWA—responsible for Palestinian refugees (as it predates UNHCR), he is a Swiss national who previously was a long-serving UN official. He came into UNRWA at a time of crisis and scandal at the leadership level. UNRWA is the largest employer outside the Palestinian government of Palestinians, writ large. While UNRWA takes a lot of criticism from Israel, without it, many more Palestinian children may have ended up in Hamas-run schools in Gaza.

- **Filippo Grandi** — The head of UNHCR is a longtime staff member of the agency he now heads. He also served as the head of UNRWA in the early 2010s. Grandi has overseen UNHCR's response to the greatest refugee crisis since World War II. He and UNHCR are essential should there be a broader escalation of the conflict.

- **Martin Griffiths** — A British career diplomat who now heads all humanitarian affairs coordination at the UN, he served as a special envoy to Yemen during the recent conflict and has built strong relationships across the region. He also launched the Center for Humanitarian Dialogue, which has facilitated a lot of back-channel diplomacy with non-state actors, including the Taliban. He has been at the helm of many conversations people do not want to have behind the scenes.

- **Cindy McCain** — The wife of the late Senator John McCain, she currently serves as the head of the World Food Programme (WFP). WFP is always at the forefront of coordinating humanitarian logistics and immediate aid. Often headed by an American (and Republican), WFP has a solid political footing in the right circles in Washington to press for a continuous humanitarian corridor during the conflict.

• **Sigrid Kaag** — A longtime United Nations official, Kaag recently served as a political party leader in her home country of the Netherlands, rising also to foreign minister in the government. The UN secretary-general appointed her in late 2023 as the senior humanitarian and reconstruction coordinator for Gaza. Her UN experience, including leadership roles on the Lebanon and Syria files, and her overall experience in the region going back several decades means she is well-versed with all parties.

Others in the United Nations structure also play important roles and are not mentioned here, particularly the networks of special representatives of the secretary-general and resident coordinators and various staff of the ICRC.

## Third Sector

The predominant actors in this crisis are those leading governments, sub-state and non-state groups, and international organizations. However, a range of private individuals and institutions of import also weigh into the conversation. This is most notable in the United States and is detailed in this section.

There are other opinion-makers, such as journalists, people with large social media followings, and religious figures, who continue to sway public sentiment. One thing to note is that a lot of Islamic organizations (religious, not political) with global reach have limited independence due to the aftermath of the War on Terror and, as such, are discounted in this analysis.

- **Think tanks** – The principal think tank to watch would be the Washington Institute for Near East Policy, which Robert Satloff heads. This is the closest proxy for the thinking within the Biden administration on Israel, even though it is to the right of most public positions of the Democratic Party. There are innumerable institutions to take note of more generally but their direct influence on this issue will be marginal.

- **Advocacy organizations** – A range of predominantly Jewish advocacy organizations have close relationships with the White House and have a wide reach in informing Israeli policy over the years. Notable ones would be the American Israel Public Affairs Committee, the American Jewish Committee, the Anti-Defamation League (ADL), and J Street. There are other organizations, such as the World Jewish Congress, but they are not as politically relevant from a policy perspective at the current moment. Jonathan Greenblatt, the head of the ADL, who served in the Obama administration, is a notable voice. Until the current crisis, there was tremendous polarization within these groups due to the Netanyahu government's planned judicial reform.

  In terms of Arab American advocacy organizations, they are less organized, established, and present. James Zogby co-founded and led the Arab American Institute. He was previously a member of the Executive Committee of the Democratic Party and has reach. The Council on American Islamic Relations ostensibly represents Muslim American interests, but its leadership is not only questionable but also has grown distant from many Muslim communities.

  There are more nascent grassroots groups not listed here that are linked to the Squad Plus world; they are not necessarily influential in centrist Democrat circles. That being said, there could be a coordinated political push given the elections in 2024 bringing such groups closer together and thus this is something to track. A similar point could be made regarding Christian Zionist groups on the other side of the political spectrum.

- **Non-profits** — In previous decades, humanitarian campaigns by non-profit organizations and leaders showing up in Washington would be the norm. This may still be the case, but most large U.S. non-profits are funded by the U.S. government. They would be unable to militate for any policy change independently and would most acutely be seeking funding from USAID.

# IV

# HISTORY

What follows is a very abridged narrative history of the chronological periods of what has become the Palestinian-Israeli conflict. This is not a replacement for reading widely; additional resources at the end of this publication list some reference points.

In Israel, there has always been a robust debate on the history of the conflict, particularly the early history. Benny Morris and Avi Shlaim (so-called New Historians in Israel) came to similar conclusions, from divergent political perspectives, about a root aspect of the conflict: Palestinians were forcibly displaced from their homes in what is today Israel. The debate now in Israel is about whether it was intentional and justified.

The above is essential to point out at the outset, as, given the politicization of history, even basic facts that are self-evident have taken decades to become widely acceptable. Nevertheless, there continue to be countless debates around red herrings. It is best to avoid those traps and accept that disputes of finer points do not take away from what is, by this point, a common understanding among most historians of the last 150 years of the conflict and its precursors.

## ORIGINS (PRE-1870s)

Israel and Palestine, as terms, go back millennia in the region, and there are significant use cases for both. The emergence of Judaism as an organized faith and Hebrew as a language happened in intersecting historical events, movements, and ideologies in the thousand years prior to the destruction of the Second Temple in Jerusalem in 70 AD. Today, much historicity is impossible to determine and is now conflated with religious tradition and reimagined memory, as with any national movement.

What is clear is that there has been a Jewish population in the areas now known as Israel and Palestine going back 2,500 years. At times, that population spoke Hebrew and, more colloquially, Aramaic (the language of Jesus), Arabic, and even Yiddish (especially in later centuries and following the pre-Zionist migration of European Jews). The Jewish population in the Holy Land varied in composition and ethnic background, whether Sephardic, Ashkenazi, Mizrahi, and so forth.

The mention of 70 AD is relevant because Israel calls the West Bank by the names Judea and Samaria today, echoing Biblical references and those from history 2,000 years ago. After subsequent wars between the Roman Empire and restive Jewish subjects and political movements, the Romans integrated Judea into a wider Roman province, essentially called Palestine (the naming nomenclature is far more complex but is kept simple here) in the second century. Again, much of this is ancient history, but the word Palestine (in whatever iteration) had been used concurrently for over 1,000 years earlier, even by Ancient Egyptians and Assyrians.

Ultimately, whatever name came first, the people who originally inhabited the land were Canaanites, and from them or alongside them emerged Israelites and whomever else inhabited the land.

Does it matter who was there when? After all, Jerusalem and the Holy Land were among the most visited places on earth. At the heart of numerous crossroads of numerous empires, it would been one of the most ethnically mixed places on Earth. During the Ottoman Empire's rule, people would have settled there from all over.

For centuries, the area was a polity of the Ottoman Empire, and the world was not neatly organized into conceptual nation-states. In the 1870s, the Ottoman district the Mutasarrifate of Jerusalem was full of multiple languages, people with varying religious denominations and many ethnic identities. However, it was predominantly Muslim and ruled as such by the Ottomans. An excellent description of Ottoman Jerusalem can be found in the travelogue of prominent Russian Diplomat Dimitri Dashkov (covered well by Theophilus C. Prousis in *Russian-Ottoman Relations in the Levant: The Dashkov Archive*).

Finally, Jerusalem, for many reasons, has had spiritual significance to Muslims and Christians of all denominations, just as for Jews, since time immemorial. The centrality varies, and each faith group's traditions intersect with Jerusalem repeatedly. However, the overall Palestinian–Israeli conflict is based mainly on bi-national narrative construction and ethnic rivalries. The religious dimension, while significant, is in fact secondary and not the driver of the conflict.

That being said, religious polarization shapes the conflict, reinforces narratives, and creates concurrent dynamics.

## ZIONIST MOVEMENT (1870s–1920s)

Before the 19th century, Jewish migration, or *Aliyah* as it is referred to in the Zionist tradition, resulted from haphazard migration, movement within the Ottoman Empire, or displacement due to persecution, such as during the 1492 Spanish Inquisition. Religiously speaking, Zionism as a concept was nearly nonexistent and was not doctrinally sound within most rabbinic circles.

In the 19th century, successive waves of Jewish migration began, such as from Russia. In the latter decades of the century, efforts became more organized and frequent, involving purchasing land and establishing new communities. Given this tide and sensing more comprehensive support, activist Theodor Herzl founded the Zionist Organization and held the First Zionist Congress in Switzerland in 1897.

From its inception, the Zionist movement was largely secular and led by secular Jews. It was not even widely accepted in the Jewish community, perhaps until the 1940s, even though there was growing momentum (the exact level of support is contestable, especially among non-Western Jewish communities).

From its inception, there were counter-currents within the Zionist movement that complemented the socialist-left leanings of many of its leaders. That counter-current, from the right, was intellectually led by Ze'ev Jabotinsky. Today, the sense of two visions for Israel and how it should conduct itself remains.

What is interesting is that even until the very moment Israel was established, there was limited religious ideology in its formation. It was motivated more by an ethnic-based nationalism for the Jewish people. There are many lengthy analyses of Zionism that explore this and all its facets. Suffice it to say that the prominent leaders of the Zionist movement, its associated organizations, and the State of Israel, when founded, were primarily Ashkenazi secular Jews.

Herzl died in 1904. The Zionist movement continued to gain momentum after his passing, especially following the Sykes-Picot Agreement in 1916 and the Balfour Declaration in 1917. Following the end of World War I and the departure of the Ottoman Empire from the scene, the Arab world was divided and atomized. The British Mandate of Palestine, in effect for 30 years following, established the modern borders of what is today Israel, including the Palestinian territories.

It is a myth that the British, from inception, sought to placate the Zionist movement. The British authorities constantly raided various Zionist groups and accused them of incitement, rebellion, and insurrection. However, the British did facilitate significant migration of Jews in the 1920s from Europe, and this led to rising rivalries and tensions with Arab communities. That being said, the British were also committed to establishing dual national homes for the Palestinians and the Jewish people within the Mandate.

Palestinian protests and riots in the early and late 1920s started to emerge due to not just tensions with the Jewish community but also to assert a nascent national identity, although mainly at this point as Arabs, not necessarily Palestinians. It was in this period that the Haganah was formed, a self-defense force of Jews (Yishuv) in Palestine.

## ARAB UPRISING (1930s) AND ZIONIST INSURGENCY (1940s)

Palestinians were loosely organized compared to Zionist organizations. Still, in the 1930s, they formed the Arab Higher Committee, primarily led by Mohammed Amin Al Husseini, who was also the Grand Mufti of Jerusalem. Soon after, organized revolts, known as the Arab Revolt in Palestine, led to strikes, mass protests, and civil violence. After this revolt, the British disbanded the Committee and exiled its leaders. With Husseini driven to exile, Palestinians were without much leadership, and some in exile found refuge with Axis powers in Europe.

The emerging Arab nationalism of the era created a pan-Arabist feeling. The sentiments driving initial Palestinian aspirations were grounded in overall dissatisfaction due to all colonial powers throughout the Arab world. Meanwhile, rising antisemitism in Europe and the growing march to war only intensified Jewish migration to Palestine.

Due to the rising discontent across all groups in Palestine, the British convened the Peel Commission, which subsequently issued the first report calling for the partition of the land and population transfer to facilitate two states. Regardless of the percentages, the type of land discussed, and so forth, the Peel Commission landed flat. It was unworkable, seemed to renege on the perception of what self-determination would have looked like—one combined state as a home for both Palestinian Arabs and Jews—and also, due to other preoccupations in Europe, became an unnecessary distraction for the British.

In the 1930s, a paramilitary organization, the Irgun, was formed by Zionist communities. The organization, unlike the Haganah, took offensive attacks against perceived threats, whether from the British or Arab communities. With World War II afoot, there was new urgency. Later, the Stern Gang, or Lehi, also formed as an even more militant outfit agitating for Jewish independence.

The targets for Irgun were often the British. The most prominent incident was the terrorist bombing of the King David Hotel in 1946, which killed dozens of civilians. A full-scale insurgency began; the end of World War II only heightened the urgency as the British still restricted Jewish migration to Palestine.

During the war itself, alliances were strange and shifting. Husseini, in exile, met with Hitler during World War II, and a famous photo still circulates to this day. However, some figures in the Zionist leadership also had significant contacts with Nazi Germany, representing a controversial side of the Zionist movement (the Haavara Agreement is covered by Yad Vashem on its website, www.yadvashem. org). There were also numerous attempted links between Lehi and Nazi Germany and then Lehi and Stalin.

## 1948 ARAB–ISRAELI WAR (1947–1949)

The modern history of Israel and Palestine begins in 1947. It is bloody, full of devastation from inception, and descends into a cascading set of conflicts that have continued to this day. Yet amidst this, the Jewish people did find a home and form a state, and that state has become one of the most prosperous countries in the world and a leader in innovation. The Palestinians, meanwhile, have been dispossessed and occupied, are still without a state, and are in continuous despair.

On November 29, 1947, the United Nations passed Resolution 181 at the General Assembly, which called for a partition of the land. This came about as the British, looking to quit the British Mandate of Palestine, referred the matter to the newly formed United Nations. A special committee led a study creating an initial roadmap for partition. The final resolution gave a Jewish state about 61% of the British Mandate with the remainder for an Arab state; Jerusalem would have international status.

It is difficult to imagine the moment today, but this occurred in the aftermath of World War II. There were hundreds of thousands of Jewish refugees still living in camps around Europe. Many of them had been displaced and had no homes to return to. Two years after the war, many of them tried to make their way to Palestine, including thousands on the SS Exodus, which British Army Destroyers intercepted. Meanwhile, every day, there were Jewish insurgent attacks on British police outposts in Palestine itself.

President Harry Truman came down firmly on the side of establishing a Jewish state from the early days. This quickly added a Cold War dynamic to the conflict, which would fuel it for decades. Part of President Truman's motivation was domestic politics. Part of it was to give a conclusion to World War II issues and allow the U.S. to focus on new threats. Whatever the case, it was clear there would be a State of Israel, which was ultimately declared on May 14, 1948.

Ten days before UN Resolution 181 codifying partition passed in November 1947, the Lehi had summarily executed the male members of the Arab Shubaki family for allegedly supporting the British. A reprisal attack took place by armed Arabs on Jewish passengers on a bus. These are just two incidents, but it was this initial spiral that led to full-blown strife in the British Mandate before Israeli independence six months later.

The intensification of violence continued through the end of the British Mandate on May 15, 1948, which was the day that Arab armies also invaded, and the crisis became a full-scale Arab–Israeli conflict at a regional level. Israel benefitted from a long-standing armed force in the Haganah. The leader of Israel, David Ben Gurion, consolidated the various Jewish militias into effectively an organized military force. Ultimately, arms shipments from countries such as Czechoslovakia became a critical lifeline for the nascent state.

Numerous details remain of great debate to this day. There appears to be a consensus that Jewish armed forces had intended to displace Palestinians in some villages, which is documented in depth by all manner of Israeli historians. In addition, biological agents were used to poison wells in some cases, for example, to make those villages uninhabitable.

Probably the single most influential dynamic early in the conflict was the Deir Yassin massacre, widely reported and acknowledged by the Jewish (or Yishuv) authorities at the time. Carried out by the Irgun and Lehi a month before Israel declared independence, over a hundred civilians were massacred in an assault on the village. This precipitated panic in the Palestinian population, many of whom fled and then were never able to return.

Another pivotal moment was an assault on a Jewish kibbutz, Kfar Etzion, by Arab irregular forces. The mass death of its inhabitants, the razing to the ground of the town, and the imprisonment in a POW camp of the survivors hardened the militant forces in Israel around the need to confront Arab armies with full force.

The Arab–Israeli War lasted for about a year. It ended with armistice agreements between Israel and Jordan, Egypt,

Syria, and Lebanon in 1949. This demarcated the State of Israel's de facto borders where they are today, and what are considered occupied territories (in the West Bank and Gaza Strip). The West Bank and East Jerusalem fell under Jordanian rule. The Gaza Strip fell under Egyptian rule.

Meanwhile, Resolution 194 in the UN General Assembly called for a return of Palestinian refugees. Wider recognition of the State of Israel at the UN occurred on May 11, 1949. No State of Palestine presented itself for recognition at the time. The conflict was still seen in the realm of a regional conflict rather than along a Palestinian-Israeli dimension.

This also was the origin of the Palestinian refugee crisis that continues up to today. UNRWA was established to manage the needs of 700,000 Palestinian refugees. That number has since swelled to close to six million registered refugees within the West Bank, Gaza, Jordan, Lebanon, and Syria. While much is contested or in dispute, it is clear and established that Palestinian refugees were blocked from returning, their land was subsequently expropriated, and many villages were razed to the ground. Other villages became the new homes of Jewish occupants.

The Arab-Israeli War ended with Arab armies effectively defeated, the Palestinians displaced and with no real strategy for the future. On the other side, Israel was established and started to form its relevant institutions. The conflict shifted in dynamic subsequently to have two fronts—regional confrontations between states and insurgent confrontations involving Palestinian guerilla groups.

## FEDAYEEN INCURSIONS AND THE SUEZ CRISIS (1950s)

Throughout the 1950s, Palestinians organized into guerrilla units called *fedayeen* and either infiltrated Israel or mounted guerilla raids. These were often sponsored by various Arab armies, who had no interest in another round of state-to-state fighting. There were dozens of casualties on the Israeli side. As a result, Israel set up the infamous Unit 101, helmed by Ariel Sharon (through which he rose to fame). It carried out multiple raids, some with military purposes and others more retributive. The most famous of these was the raid on the town of Qibya in the West Bank in 1953, which itself was condemned by UN Security Council Resolution 100 due to the extent of civilian devastation.

By 1956, Israel was feeling especially strong, and with Cold War lines being drawn, it allied with the British and French to conduct the Suez War in response to the nationalization of the Suez Canal by then–Egyptian President Gamal Abdel Nassar. The war lasted a week and resulted in everyone withdrawing to the 1949 armistice lines. The Suez Canal remained under Egyptian control, an outcome principally due to the United States backing of Egypt's stance.

The aftermath, though, demonstrated Israeli superiority over surrounding Arab armies. It also was a prelude to the same acquisition of territory (the Gaza Strip, Sinai, East Jerusalem, West Bank, and Golan Heights) set to occur just a decade later in the 1967 War. The subsequent era became one of tremendous Arab nationalism and pan-Arabism as the ideology of the day. Nasser's philosophy reigned supreme, and the Ba'ath Party was emerging in other countries, such as Syria and Iraq. Syria and Egypt united to form one country for several years, called the United Arab Republic, during this time.

Overall, Nasser effectively promoted republicanism over monarchism. This is important to note because an inherent clash emerged between republicans and monarchists between countries in the region, which continued into the 1970s. It meant the region was very much divided in any consensus approach to the Arab world, which consequently affected the Palestinian issue.

## SIX DAY WAR AND AFTERMATH (1967)

By 1967, Israel had become a cause célèbre in the Western world. Its success was undeniable. As a state of refugees who had escaped the worst conditions in Europe, all political stripes celebrated it.

John F. Kennedy remarked on the American view at a convention of the Zionist Organization of America in 1960: "Friendship for Israel is not a partisan matter. It is a national commitment."

Martin Luther King, Jr. reinforced this intention to the Rabbinical Assembly in New York in 1968: "I see Israel, and [I] never mind saying it, as one of the great outposts of democracy in the world, and a marvelous example of what can be done, how desert land almost can be transformed into an oasis of brotherhood and democracy."

For the Palestinians, there was a feeling of abandonment and no true political representation. Fatah and the Palestine Liberation Organization were formed in this vacuum. Fatah was founded in Kuwait by Yasser Arafat and several comrades around 1960. One of his earliest supporters was Mahmoud Abbas. The PLO was formally announced at the Arab League Summit in 1964 to become the overarching group representing Palestinians within historic Palestine and refugees outside. Yet, initially, it was still heavily influenced by Egyptian interests.

In 1967, Israel launched a war against surrounding Arab countries that became widely known as a humiliation. It altered forever the Arab scene, emasculated pan-Arabism, and laid the groundwork for the modern Middle East and the nature of the Palestinian struggle henceforth.

In six days, Israel captured the Golan Heights from Syria, the West Bank and East Jerusalem from Jordan, and the Gaza Strip from Egypt. In fact, by the end of the conflict, Israel had also seized the entirety of the Sinai Peninsula from Egypt, which it finally returned in 1982.

The war also laid the grounds for Israeli administrative integration of East Jerusalem and the Golan Heights and an occupation framework for the Gaza Strip and the West Bank. A new wave of Palestinian refugees fled across the territories and region. The war ended with UN Security Council Resolution 242, which stipulated that seized territory would be returned.

This moment represented the fulfillment of *Eretz Israel*. It was doubly reinforced by a final exodus of Jews from many Arab countries. Until 1967, a sizable Jewish population had remained in leading cities throughout the region, where they had been for centuries. This further reinforced Israel's position as the one homeland for the global Jewry.

After this war, the PLO solidified itself and its role. The defeat of Arab armies led to resistance activity against Israel. This was when more radical factions began to engage in terrorism as a tactic. The PLO was taken over by Yasser Arafat and associated militant factions, notably Fatah. Many of the subsequent guerrilla attacks originated from Jordanian territory. Each successful attack led to a surge in recruitment for Fatah worldwide.

There was, however, an overflowing set of militant groups, many of them socialist-inspired. The global mood was one of revolution and anti-colonialism. Palestinian militants forged transnational ideological identities and alliances as a result. Outside of Fatah, the Popular Front for the Liberation of Palestine and the Democratic Front for the Liberation of Palestine were active. They were both helmed by Christians, who constituted a large part of the Palestinian diaspora.

The PFLP was notably hostile to the Jordanian monarchy. Tensions mounted between the PLO (the umbrella organization for most of these factions) and the Jordanians, and raids into Israeli territory brought Israeli airstrikes into Jordan. By 1970, the situation was unsalvageable. King Hussein of Jordan's motorcade came under attack by PLO militants. This was also when the PFLP started hijackings of aircraft globally, bringing one of them to Jordan with dramatic effect when the plane (sans hostages) was blown up on the tarmac.

That September, now known as Black September, the monarchy took action to begin to expel the PLO and various factions from Jordan. Thousands of Palestinians were killed as a result, including many civilians. In response to all of this, Jordan moved closer to Israel.

The Amman agreement between the Jordanian monarchy and the PLO led to the relocation of the PLO's base of operations to South Lebanon, including the relocation of most fighters. It also led to irrecoverable distrust between the PLO and all Arab governments, which continued throughout Arafat's life. One group that emerged from all this was the Black September Organization. This group became one of the more radical in the region, assassinating, for example, a Jordanian prime minister and carrying out the notorious Munich Olympic massacre.

## YOM KIPPUR WAR AND CAMP DAVID ACCORDS (1970s)

By the early 1970s, it was clear that Arab states wanted to move on from the conflict. Henry Kissinger, across different appointments, played a notable role in the U.S. government during this period. The Yom Kippur War in 1973 laid the groundwork for the subsequent Camp David Accords. In a grand strategic view, the U.S. used its role in 'saving' Israel to pressure it to make a deal with Arab countries for long-term peace.

On Yom Kippur, October 7, 1973, Arab armies led by Syria and Egypt launched a surprise attack on Israel. The war lasted nearly three weeks. The campaign was led by relatively newly installed President Anwar Sadat in Egypt and Syria by President Hafez Al Assad. Golda Meir was Israel's prime minister, and ultimately, the war led to significant disgrace for her within Israel, and subsequently resigned. Her successor was Yitzhak Rabin, who played an instrumental role in peace negotiations in later years.

While Israel did suffer losses in the initial days, by the end of the war it had lost no territory and had progressed even further within both Egypt and Syria. However, this was only possible because Kissinger and Nixon had pushed for and facilitated significant rearmament of Israel during the conflict. This brought the specter of Cold War tensions to the fore, which prompted the cease-fire negotiations in haste. The war was ended through U.S. negotiations and codified in UNSC Resolution 338.

The aftermath of the war brought home to Israel that regional peace was in its interest. In addition, the short-lived Saudi-led OPEC oil embargo from 1973 to 1974 also created global urgency around resolution. Although King Faisal of Saudi Arabia, who spearheaded this move, was dead by 1975, the United States continued to work in earnest across administrations toward peace accords.

The Camp David Accords, facilitated by President Jimmy Carter, were reached between Israel and Egypt in 1978 (and 1979), which enabled the return of the Sinai Peninsula to Egypt. The Camp David Accords had two components, one between Egypt and Israel and another around self-determination for Palestinians in the occupied territories. Ultimately, the second was never realized. Egyptian President Sadat himself was assassinated in 1981 by militants opposed to the Accords.

There were many unresolved issues from the negotiations. Regionally, the status of the Golan Heights remained open, but in 1981, Israel stated that it would integrate the Golan into its state and began settling it. PLO factions grew stronger and more emboldened in Lebanon as the Camp David Accords brought no resolution to the Palestinian issue.

In 1979, Israel and the U.S. lost an ostensible ally in Tehran when the Islamic Revolution overthrew the Shah. The inability to fully resolve the overall Palestinian-Israeli conflict would mean the end of one era and the beginning of another by the end of the decade.

## LEBANON INVASION (1982)

By 1982, the PLO was again running a proto-state. This time, it was in Lebanon instead of Jordan. In the early days of the Lebanese civil war in 1975, the PLO was involved in running battles with the Kataeb and various Christian militias (and also Shiite groups in the South) in Lebanon. It naturally allied with the Muslim-Left-Arabist side of the civil war. Israel provided support to the groups fighting the PLO.

A range of incidents occurred during the war, which arguably was even instigated by the PLO presence; notable among them was the battle and massacre at the Palestinian refugee camp, Tel Al Zaatar. After that, there was no real turning back for tensions between the PLO and the other side of the civil war in the country. The South Lebanese Army (SLA), a Christian militia, was the preeminent ally of Israel in the country and received significant funding. It acted as a proxy for Israel in the late 1970s and early 1980s.

The situation was untenable. PLO factions continued to conduct raids on Israel originating from Lebanon. One of the more infamous attacks was by Samir Kuntar, who kidnapped and killed two Israeli hostages, a father and his daughter, after landing by boat in Israel. Kuntar was imprisoned and not released until decades later in a prisoner exchange with Hezbollah.

In 1982, Israel confidently invaded Lebanon and laid siege to Beirut. Divisions within the PLO, between Palestinian factions, and the overall fighting between various Lebanese and Palestinian groups meant that the PLO had an unsustainable position in the country. Within a few months, the PLO relocated many of its fighters outside the country, and its political headquarters migrated to Tunis.

Very quickly, Israel realized it had gotten more than it bargained for. Lebanese (and somewhat Israeli-allied) President Bachir Gemayal was assassinated in September by unknown groups. Then, several days later, militias associated with his political party committed the Sabra and Shatila massacre under the direct supervision of the IDF and Israel's Defense Minister Ariel Sharon, who had flown into Beirut to conduct operations following the assassination.

The claim was that there were remnants of the PLO in the Lebanese town of Sabra and the Palestinian camp of Shatila and that the PLO was responsible for President Gemayal's assassination (although today, the killing is seemingly attributed to Syrian agents). Whatever the accusations, over 2,000 men, women, and children lay dead at the end of a two-day killing spree.

Less than two weeks after the massacre, Israel established the Kahan Commission to investigate. The situation in Lebanon was going from bad to worse. The messiness of Israeli involvement in Lebanon meant that it soon withdrew from Beirut to a security corridor in the South, empowering its allies in the SLA. It had achieved the withdrawal of the PLO, ostensibly, in any case.

Yet, at the same time the PLO was declining in relevance and presence in Lebanon, the Iranian Revolutionary Guard Corps had set up a base in the country. The militias of the Amal faction (from Shiite communities) were battling heavily with Palestinians in a battle for the refugee camps, and this internecine approach left an opening within Lebanon's Shiite community for mobilization.

The U.S. presence in Lebanon, formally to restore stability to the country as part of a multinational force, gave way to new vulnerabilities in a new Middle East. The 1983 Embassy and then Marine Barracks bombings were significant events for the U.S., leading to hundreds of deaths. Whether it was Hezbollah (just forming at the time), Islamic Jihad Organization (a group that may have existed in name only), or the IRGC directly, they marked the start of a series of significant attacks and campaigns. Assassinations, such as that of Malcolm Kerr, NBA Coach Steve Kerr's father and then president of the American University of Beirut, became a regular occurrence. Hostage-taking in Beirut, especially of Americans, became the norm.

Hezbollah emerged formally during this time in the 1980s. It represented quite a sea change because previously in South Lebanon there had been significant hostility to Palestinian militias due to their brazenness. It took Israel's invasion to create Hezbollah, the most potent anti-Israeli adversary in the region.

In the 1980s, Hezbollah had as much focus on battling rival militias in Lebanon and running attacks on Western targets as it did on fighting Israel. It was only in the 1990s, and particularly after the assassination of its secretary-general Abbas Al Musawi in 1992, that it became an exclusive, organized, and supremely effective fighting force against Israel.

### FIRST INTIFADA (LATE 1980s) AND OSLO ACCORDS (1990s)

The rising tide of Islamism as an organizing ideology within the Arab world seemed only natural with increasing religiosity and a failure of pan-Arabism. The Islamic Revolution in Iran gave inspiration to both Sunni and Shiite Islamists. There were reverberating agitations across the Arab world, notably in Egypt and Syria. In Egypt, following the assassination of President Sadat, there was a severe crackdown on the Muslim Brotherhood. In Syria, following a low-level insurgency by the Muslim

Brotherhood, Syrian President Hafez Al Assad led a massacre in Hama in 1982 of thousands.

The Palestinian issue was similarly susceptible to these shifts. Hamas, which means zeal in Arabic, is an acronym for *Harakat Al Muqawama Al Islamiyia*, or the movement of Islamic resistance. It grew out of an offshoot of the Muslim Brotherhood, originally a charity called the Islamic Center. That charity was not just tolerated and recognized but tacitly supported by Israel.

In the early 1980s, in the Palestinian territories, the precursor to Hamas was seen as the lesser of two evils by Israel's security establishment. In an era where the *mujahideen* were fighting the Soviets and secular ideology, it made sense to support Islamic 'zeal' to oppose the socialist, secularist PLO.

Hamas was officially founded in 1987, and its charter was launched in 1988. Israel itself only outlawed Hamas in 1989 after an attack on Israeli soldiers. It was a time of shifts. The Cold War was ending, and Islamic militants were losing their usefulness to the West. Ultimately, these groups turned their attention globally to the new greater enemy, the United States.

The First Intifada was a game changer for the conflict that had gone from regional to hyper-local. Every neighboring country had been neutralized, cordoned, or invaded, and yet here was Israel still facing a threat, now emerging from the restive Palestinian territories under its occupation. Initially, it was a nonviolent civil disobedience movement consisting of riots, barricades, and stone-throwing.

The images echoed around the world. Teenagers with slingshots and stones were facing off against tanks. The IDF met the uprising with overwhelming force. In subsequent years, some militant activities by Palestinians grew as part of the Intifada, but with low levels of violence.

During the First Intifada, the Arab League recognized the PLO as the official administrative authority in the West Bank, and Jordan withdrew its claim of presence in and financial support for the West Bank. The PLO took advantage of the global shifts and the First Intifada and, amidst somewhat fading relevance, in 1988, recognized for the first time the existence of Israel and accepted the premise of a two-state solution.

This political moment, however, was precarious. By 1991, the PLO had lost the support of many Gulf countries when it opposed the U.S. in the Gulf War. Notably, Kuwait expelled many Palestinian officials and their families.

There was a sense of momentum for peace by the early 1990s, but it was unclear what the outcome would be. The Gulf War had inflamed tensions in the Middle East when the U.S. was trying to assert its role in leading a Pax Americana. The United States was making broad attempts to 'close' files pending from the Cold War. Negotiations to end apartheid in South Africa, for example, began in earnest in 1990. The Palestinian–Israeli conflict was natural to be on the docket for the then-Bush administration.

An international peace conference was organized in Madrid in 1991, bringing informal representatives of the PLO and Israel together for the first time. These discussions laid the groundwork for the Oslo Accords. The Oslo Accords, signed in 1993 and 1995 between Yasser Arafat and Yitzhak Rabin and under Bill Clinton's supervision, focused on the situation in the Palestinian territories. The framework was based on UN Resolutions 242 and 338 and a two-state solution.

The Oslo Accords were opposed by many Palestinian militant factions as well as intellectuals. In Israel, there was vehement opposition due to what would be a death knell of *Eretz Israel*. In the backdrop of the Accords, in 1994, Jewish extremists led by Baruch Goldstein conducted an attack that massacred nearly 30 civilians in prayer at a mosque in Hebron. This led to reprisal attacks by Hamas, which began to engage in direct terrorism against civilians as a tactic. This would become its norm for the years to come.

In 1995, Israeli Prime Minister Yitzhak Rabin was assassinated by Jewish extremists who opposed the Oslo Accords. This marked a turning point for the so-called peace process. The Palestinian Authority formed by the Oslo Accords was to be in charge of the Palestinian territories. The PA, however, had limited control and was relegated only to Area A in the West Bank (i.e., less than 20% of the territory). By the mid- to late 1990s, there was growing tension between PLO factions (that ran the PA) and Hamas.

Meanwhile, in Israel, a right-wing moment brought Prime Minister Benjamin Netanyahu to power in 1996. Netanyahu, while progressing with elements of the Oslo Accords, stalled for time. Israeli settlements grew overall during the Accords, and there were 100,000 more Israeli settlers in the Palestinian territories by the end of the decade compared to 1993. Hamas also continued attacking Israeli civilian targets, including in the heart of Tel Aviv.

It is remarkable then that in the late 1990s, Ehud Barak came to power as prime minister. He quickly initiated the Israeli withdrawal from South Lebanon after 18 years of occupation. In 2000, a Camp David Summit was held between Yasser Arafat and Ehud Barak. However, the mood was dark back home for both leaders. Arafat faced an impatient Palestinian population disillusioned with the peace process. Barak faced a new threat from the right in the form of Likud leader Ariel Sharon.

If this was a proper multi-year negotiation, it may have led to a negotiated settlement. One of the criticisms from Edward Said, the prominent Palestinian intellectual, of the Oslo Accords was that they established an end without any clear endgame in mind. Many of the conflict's core issues were left to that 2000 meeting to be discussed for the first time. By the time the parties met again in Sharm El-Sheikh in October of that year, it was already too late due to what would become the Second Intifada.

There have been many books and articles written about why the negotiations failed and who was to blame, notably by former U.S. officials Robert Malley and Dennis Ross, for example. However, ultimately, regional events overtook the negotiations. The negotiations continued through Taba, Egypt, in January 2001, but political transitions were already underway in the U.S. and Israel by then. The deal discussed in Taba is the closest to what a final status could look like.

## SECOND INTIFADA (2000s)

The Taba Summit in January 2001 coincided with a new American president coming to the fore. Just two weeks later, Ehud Barak lost decisively an election to hardliner Ariel Sharon. And this was all in the midst of the outbreak of the Second Intifada, which itself was triggered in September 2000 by a visit of Sharon to the Temple Mount/Al Aqsa Mosque compound, an apparent provocation. Then, later in 2001, with the 9/11 attacks, it was clear that fighting terrorism would outweigh any concessions for peace.

The failure of the Oslo Accords sent the Palestinian issue into an abyss. The First Intifada was a natural, pan-Palestinian uprising that was largely nonviolent and pushed toward a Palestinian path for self-determination from within the territories for the first time. The Second Intifada was an uprising of anger, exasperation, and desperation. There was no clear plan. The old political guard was dying. It was the rise of Palestinian militancy in the territories and the cementing of Israeli intransigence.

The early 2000s created a clear preference for Israel in terms of a solution to the Palestinian problem: containment. With the Second Intifada raging, the Bush administration marginalized Yasser Arafat and anointed Mahmoud Abbas the key interlocuter for negotiations on behalf of the PLO. Hamas conducted dozens of suicide bombing attacks during the Second Intifada, but the Fatah-linked Al Aqsa Martyrs Brigades carried out several attacks as well.

Israel was crushing dissent and militant groups alike in the Palestinian territories, leading to thousands of deaths. With the Iraq War in full swing, the Middle East was a powder keg. President Bush managed to work alongside Sharon to engage in what was called the Roadmap to Peace as a last effort to establish a Palestinian state. When Arafat died in 2004, Mahmoud Abbas was elected President. That now represents the last moment of consolidated leadership within the Palestinian territories.

Ariel Sharon had evolved to be a realist and recognized that governing Palestinians in Gaza was not in the interest of Israel's demographic future. He withdrew from Gaza unilaterally in 2005, becoming the first prime minister to dismantle settlements. He was attacked from the right, mainly by Benjamin Netanyahu from within his Likud

Party. As such, Sharon formed a new party, Kadima, to continue on the path.

Through the 2000s, under Sharon's tenure, Israeli settlements continued to grow in the West Bank. Ariel Sharon went into a coma in early 2006 due to a stroke. His successor in Kadima and as prime minister, Ehud Olmert, continued negotiations on the Palestinian file, but the peace process effectively suffered a slow collapse. Overall, the Bush policy in the region was also failing, with the war in Iraq a complete disaster.

The Second Intifada had given way, after Arafat's death, to an intra-Palestinian conflict for political supremacy. Hamas first came to power in the 2006 Palestinian elections. While they initially formed a government, both Israel and the United States forced its collapse and blocked donors from collaborating with or funding it. An attempted unity government between Fatah and Hamas in 2007 failed, and all-out civil strife soon broke out, particularly in Gaza.

There are a lot of allegations about the involvement of the CIA in the events of 2007 and also the particular role played by Fatah strongman Mohammed Dahlan. Suffice it to say, dozens were killed, and by the end of a bloody week in June 2007, Hamas controlled Gaza and the Palestinian territories were effectively split into two. There have not been Palestinian elections since 2005 for the presidency and 2006 for the parliament. Subsequent efforts to form a unity government and reconciliation have failed, notably in 2014 and again in subsequent years.

The PA, under Fatah, consolidated its hold in the West Bank and Hamas established its dominance in the Gaza Strip, stifled any dissent, and it has remained that way since.

## LEBANON WAR (2006)

The July War in 2006 with Hezbollah redefined how Israel viewed the Palestinian–Israeli conflict, once again restoring its regional dimension. The July War established very little change on the ground. By the early 2000s, Israel had already withdrawn from most of South Lebanon, barring a few outposts. At the height of American–Iranian tensions, the July War was a re-regionalization of the conflict.

The intense month-long war, precipitated by a cross-border raid by Hezbollah, saw massive destruction across Lebanon and the displacement of hundreds of thousands. Over a thousand civilians died, but what was remarkable was that Hezbollah managed to inflict substantial military casualties on the Israeli side. Thousands of Hezbollah rockets also hit northern Israel. Overall, the situation reframed the threat that Israel faced.

While the conflict, which ended under UNSC Resolution 1701, had not flared up again to any intensity, it left an indelible mark on both parties, neither of whom want to reopen the front. It is thought that Hezbollah's capabilities are far more potent today than in 2006. Meanwhile, it is much less popular in Lebanon itself, and the July War led many Lebanese to question Hezbollah's unilateral ability to take the country to war.

For Israel, the July War meant that it began to see Iran as a clear and real threat. Iran has continued to have strong operational links with Hezbollah. Later, during the Syrian civil war in the 2010s, Hezbollah worked in tandem with the IRGC to support the Assad government. This, as mentioned prior, lessened Hezbollah's popularity back in Lebanon. Nevertheless, it brought it closer to Iran and enhanced its operational capabilities. This also established a clear resistance axis, linking Iraqi militias as well with Hezbollah and potentially other actors.

## GAZA WARS (2009, 2014, 2021)

The July War raised the specter of what Hamas could become, especially with Iranian support. It also laid the ground for Israel's policy, which sought to isolate and degrade Hamas but ultimately not eliminate it, just as with Hezbollah in Lebanon. This became the underlying pattern for Israel in the Gaza wars of the last 15 years, as outlined in Chapter II and further explored in this section.

After 2007, Hamas began to consolidate its hold on Gaza. When Barack Obama was about to assume the presidency, and amidst a deterioration of an Egyptian negotiated truce, Israel launched airstrikes, a naval bombardment, and then a sustained ground invasion. The Gaza Strip was still under a total blockade put in place after the capture of Israeli soldier Gilad Shalit in 2006.

The 2008–2009 Gaza War was relatively brutal but also short-lived, lasting three weeks. In the end, Israel felt comfortable that it had degraded Hamas's capabilities and re-established deterrence capabilities. Shortly after this round of conflict, Netanyahu became prime minister again and would stay in the position for the next decade. In 2011, Israel entered into a prisoner exchange with Hamas for Shalit.

In 2012, Hamas abandoned its offices in Syria, where it had maintained its headquarters and where Khaled Meshaal had found a home since Israel's assassination attempt on him in Jordan (and subsequent pressure) led him to flee Amman in the late 1990s. While it continued to have relations with Iran, unlike Hezbollah, Hamas had operational independence from Tehran. Hamas relocated its offices at that time to NATO member Turkey and Qatar.

Egypt had coordinated intermittent cease-fires between Hamas and Israel in the years before the 2014 Gaza War. In fact, for 18 months before the war, there was limited rocket fire into Israel from Gaza. The Netanyahu-led Israeli government launched the 2014 Gaza War in response to the kidnapping of three Israeli civilians in the West Bank. The month-long war was particularly destructive and led to over 2,000 dead Palestinians, mostly civilians. In retrospect, the war laid the groundwork for a long-term détente between Israel and Hamas.

It also showed the growing efficacy of the Iron Dome, thus creating a perception of security through technology for Israel. The Iron Dome, developed by Israel with funding from the United States, became a priority following the 2006 War with Hezbollah. While operational in 2011, the Iron Dome proved effective in 2014, but its accuracy has since dramatically improved, and nearly a decade later, it is seen as a technological game changer for Israel.

Subsequently, Egypt led successive rounds of truce talks indirectly between Hamas and Israel. It also facilitated on-and-off-again reconciliation talks between Fatah and Hamas, with some agreements coming into place in 2017. Hamas also entered into security partnerships with the Egyptian security forces to combat ISIS-linked groups. Meanwhile, Qatar began to fund the civil administration of Gaza. Israel worked with Qatar in 2018 to facilitate cash infusions into the Gaza Strip.

Despite all the political machinations and movements, the situation on the ground for Palestinians remained unresolved. Without any process or vision and with a sclerotic or divided leadership, Palestinians in the territories faced continued stagnation. This desperation, in the face of growing settlements in the West Bank, continued house demolitions, and the continuing blockade in Gaza, still did not seem to be leading to a third intifada. All the provocations, including by Israeli forces at Al Aqsa Mosque, seemed to have a waning effect. Either Palestinian factions were disorganized and demoralized or lacked popular support to wage any sustained campaign against Israel. The 10-day Hamas–Gaza battle in 2021 seemed to be an aberration, with both sides asserting their mutual deterrence as the Biden administration came to power. Egypt quickly negotiated a cease-fire.

Yet, shortly after that short flare-up, planning must have begun for the massive raid by Hamas into Israel on October 7, 2023. It calls into question the assumptions of the decade of détente (with intermittent flare-ups) negotiated by Israel under Netanyahu with Hamas.

## 'NEW MIDDLE EAST' (2020s)

When the Biden administration began its term, it wanted to eschew the centrality of the Middle East in American foreign policy. President Obama had tried to focus on a reset with Russia (that failed) and a Pivot to Asia (that was not completed) rather than concentrate on the Middle East. The Arab Spring moment and the rise of ISIS completely derailed that approach. One of the centerpieces of the Obama foreign policy approach became the Iran nuclear deal.

When President Trump came to power, he directly confronted ISIS, decapitating its leadership (by killing ISIS leader Baghdadi) and removing the group from nearly all its territorial control. He allowed Russia to operate in Syria, downgrading the U.S. presence in the country.

He also signaled a U.S. withdrawal further afield from Afghanistan. Meanwhile, he sought to re-isolate Iran and link the rest of the region into a security architecture.

In this context of strategic maneuvering, Trump's team led the development of the Abraham Accords in 2020, which were quite remarkable. They brought three Arab countries, Morocco, UAE, and Bahrain, into normalization with Israel. There were whispers of dozens of other contacts with Muslim countries looking to follow suit. All this was welcomed by the Netanyahu government in Israel. Ultimately, Iran was being isolated and Israel was normalizing without having to sacrifice anything on the Palestinian issue.

Hamas was also relatively content during this time. In effect, its ties with Iran and Syria had deteriorated. Under the Netanyahu–Trump era, Hamas was de facto tolerated and strengthened. Its leadership was living unencumbered in Qatar. By the time the Biden administration came along, the White House was more than happy to pursue a policy of non-engagement on the Palestinian file.

National Security Advisor Jake Sullivan wrote an article, "The Sources of American Power" in *Foreign Affairs* November/December 2023 issue, released just before the October 7 attacks (and subsequently revised). He outlined the Biden administration's views on the conflict:

"Although the Middle East remains beset with perennial challenges, the region is quieter than it has been for decades… The Israeli-Palestinian situation is tense, particularly in the West Bank. Still, in the face of serious frictions, we have de-escalated crises in Gaza and restored direct diplomacy between the parties after years of its absence."

Sullivan had relegated the management of the Middle East on the National Security Council to Brett McGurk and instead focused on the Saudi–Israel normalization deal, building on Trump's Abraham Accords. The idea was that Hamas was contained, diplomatic channels were open with everyone (including Iran), and that Israel and America felt secure in the region.

The year 2023 had already been a deadly one for Palestinians in the West Bank compared to any other year in almost a decade. As described previously, under the surface, issues had accumulated for years, and there was palpable discontent in the air.

In Israel, never-before-seen street protests effectively divided the country into two camps. The judiciary had long played an independent role in the heavily polarized country. The Netanyahu government challenged that independence when it returned to power in late 2022. A new judicial reform had been put forward to this effect. Israel seemed to be facing an internal existential moment.

## OCTOBER 7 AND THE AFTERMATH

This was the history of the conflict before October 7, 2023. The more immediate history of what led to October 7 has yet to be captured. When did Hamas start planning, and what was the role of Iran in its support? How and why did Israeli security forces fail so completely that day? To what extent is October 7 part of a broader Palestinian uprising? Is Hamas simply a proxy for other interests, unlike in the first and second intifadas?

This will all be heavily investigated one day when the crisis and conflict, now unfolding, subside.

There are always more questions than answers.

# V

# THE WAY FORWARD

*"The arc of the moral universe is long*
*but it bends toward justice."*
— Martin Luther King Jr
(Washington DC | March 31, 1968)

The famed civil rights leader uttered these famous words a number of times, including in the week before he was assassinated. The arc of the moral universe may be long, but these days, it is unclear when it will bend toward justice. Conflicts seem intractable. Problems persist indefinitely. Nowhere is this despair more entrenched than in the proverbial Holy Land.

Nearly eight decades on, nothing but more death and destruction seems on offer. Palestinians remain dispossessed and occupied, without a state in a world of states. Israelis sense they will never be secure from violence. Every issue between Israel and the Palestinians is unresolved. The events of October 7 and the aftermath have only solidified the feeling that there is no end in sight for all parties.

Where is the moral arc? Where do movements for change come from if one is in Palestine or Israel or seeking to effect change there? Where are the *new* ideas?

Ultimately, the only realistic pathway forward is for organic ideas and *ideamakers* to emerge and take root within the Holy Land.

It would have been difficult to see new thinking originating from within Israel before October 7, 2023. In South Africa, the existential threat of an end of apartheid led to a new paradigm of thinking for the White elite in the country. In that sense, the October 7 attacks may inadvertently bring new ideas to the fore in Israel about the way forward. Some will be dark, but there may be a sliver of light.

While many Palestinians may want to wait for the emerging East and South, the post-October 7 aftermath shows that these broad swaths of geography lack the confidence or dynamism to mobilize material support with resonance (beyond symbolism). This may change, but it does not appear to be on the horizon. It may mean that the notion of a two-state solution, considered a moribund idea in many Palestinian political circles, has renewed life.

## THE DAY AFTER IN GAZA

Ultimately, Israel will fall short of its goal of removing Hamas through military actions. It may have made a severe mistake in undertaking sustained military action immediately on October 7. It could have built a War on Terror–style coalition. After the 9/11 attacks, America waited nearly a month before invading Afghanistan on October 7, 2001 (coincidentally, the same date).

Many analysts pointed out at the outset that Israel had unrealistic objectives and no endgame. Thus, Israel has been caught in an unending assault and deployment of military means. While Hamas's capabilities have been degraded, and the collective punishment will assuredly have a deterrence effect, the goal of Hamas dismantlement will not be achieved militarily.

The continuing waterfall of destruction and loss of Palestinian life is similarly untenable. In addition to a moral stain and humanitarian catastrophe, it will also create generational blowback. There is a point of no return that Israel could cross, where it will jeopardize significant prospects for any regional cooperation. With this in mind, Western powers, notably the United States, have been looking to pull Israel back from a point of no return, even if they have not mandated de-escalation.

It appears that for any long-term cease-fire, the United States has a stated objective that a new Palestinian government will be installed in the Gaza Strip. In addition, there would be some type of negotiation to ensure Hamas would no longer be formally present in the territory. That would mean that any formal appearance by Hamas, militarily or politically, could be met by Israeli counteractions.

With this in mind, how can deeper progress towards a lasting solution be brought about the day after, and what should various parties do to bring it about (Palestinians, Israelis, regional actors, the United States, and others)?

It appears that the sequence of steps required the day after the violence subsides is as follows:

1) **Ensure a definitive end to the current crisis (easier said than done)** — There needs to be a grand bargain put on the table by regional powers in conjunction with the United States, including a full hostage and prisoner exchange and removal of political and military control by the current Hamas apparatus in Gaza. This was Hamas's reality prior to 2006, and the group can still evolve in that context.

2) **Consolidate a Palestinian authority (either the PA or another new body)** — Israeli forces will have to withdraw fully (or at the very least partially) from the Gaza Strip. Israel is not prepared for a full re-occupation, and this would, in any case, be a bad strategic idea. Neither regional forces nor American authorities would like to play this role. Thus, it falls on the Palestinian Authority, or a new form of the Palestinian Authority, to play this role in both Gaza and the West Bank. Regional and Western governments are already preparing for this.

3) **Enable a post-Hamas Hamas** — No scenario ends with Hamas staying as it is, either in power or in its current form. Yet, there is also no scenario in which Hamas disappears. It has a multi-decade presence within the Palestinian population. There must be an off-ramp for the movement and its members. The best approach would be enabling a new body with only a social and political frame to have legitimate status, akin to Sinn Féin.

Of course, some in Israel may object, but that is not a realistic objection. There is no de-Baathification to come (and historically that has not worked). The open question will be about its leadership, which will most likely need to relocate to an alternate country from Qatar. For the United States, it is better to have Hamas leadership in a Western-oriented country rather than Iran. A backdoor deal with Damascus could allow Hamas to return to Syria with heavy restrictions on activity.

4) **Choose one of the existing Palestinian leaders** — While a Palestinian authority can be empowered perfunctorily, the current leadership would need to be updated. This can be done through fiat, elections, or simply rerouting funding. Two clear options, neither of them

necessarily tenable, are often raised: Mohammed Dahlan or Marwan Barghouti (the former a strongman more palatable to Israel, the latter a militant populist favored by Palestinians). With time and an open political process, a third alternative could emerge. In the interim, a figure like Mustafa Barghouti could oversee a transition. But falling back to a technocratic hope could simply lead to a new Hamas taking the space a weak leader offers.

5) **Project demilitarized power of the Palestinians** — With an expanded Palestinian authority under new leadership, it would be important to expand its force projection. Ultimately, that force projection cannot threaten Israel but needs to develop a monopoly of force in the urban centers under its control. The security apparatus in the West Bank already operates in this manner.

6) **Foster elections for the parliament and presidency** — There will be flagging legitimacy if the prior steps do not lead to new elections that allow for legitimated political representation across the board with the consent of Palestinians. This has not happened since 2006 (in terms of the parliament). This may or may not lead to a new Palestinian leader outside the ones mentioned. It will confirm and cement the anointed leader's status through electoral legitimacy.

7) **Invest in reconstruction, development, and growth** — In addition to more immediate aid and recovery efforts, there will need to be long-term investment in reconstruction, development, and growth that gives a positive view of the emerging Palestinian leadership, authority, and dynamic. Without this, alternative and/ or rejectionist forces will take root. This mechanism must be administered by an international institution

or a similar body (regarding reconstruction and development). It cannot be subject to the daily whims of Israeli security authorities or border controls; the latter perhaps should be handled by regional parties.

## PIPE DREAMS FOR PEACE

Where do these seven steps take the conflict? Back to 1999, 2005, 2015, or back to October 6, 2023? These steps, already perhaps unrealistic, would still be insufficient. This is obvious to even the casual observer. And that is why pipe dreams for peace are part of the realpolitik scenario. There is no sustainable status quo without the pipe dream of dual self-determination for both Israel and Palestine.

The glaring absence of any organized political Palestinian advocacy in light of the aftermath of the October 7 attacks shows how lacking the current leadership and organizational elements of the official Palestinian apparatus are. While reform can come from within, it is hard to see the PLO, PA, or any successor body standing on their own globally and having the dynamic resonance to militate for the Palestinian position and change.

### A Palestinian Collective

The Palestinian diaspora and partisans have filled the vacuum in media, social media, public squares, and political offices left by the PLO and PA. While that energy can be positive, it is low-return if not cultivated to full effect. It can also be ignored by official actors. Thus, just like the Jewish community and Zionist movements before 1947, the Palestinian diaspora may need to enact a new organized body representing its apolitical interests.

While the PLO perhaps is akin to the World Zionist Organization and the PA to the various bodies representing the Yishuv, another representative organization could still emerge. In 1936, the World Jewish Congress was founded. This body effectively advocates for Jewish minorities around the world. A novel Palestinian organization that advocates for Palestinian communities across the globe, harnesses their energies, and is present at advocacy moments is currently absent.

This challenging undertaking falls on the Palestinian diaspora: to forge a new Palestinian Collective that can become the largest organization representing Palestinian interests globally. It could, in effect, also become independent from political interests and be funded by the Palestinian diaspora, which has significant wealth today.

The Palestinian Collective could have its own humanitarian arm and easily generate hundreds of millions of dollars of aid for Palestinians rather than relying on existing organizations. It could create a media department with its own publications rather than depending on traditional media. It could have a scholarship program and help bring about a new generation of Palestinian leaders. It could have its own advocacy platform and help fund political support in Western capitals. It could have a global engagement body and convey the Palestinian perspective to stakeholders in the Middle East, parallel to the PA or PLO.

Whether through the Palestinian Collective or another organized effort, the Palestinian diaspora, burdensome as it seems, may also need to launch a dramatic push à la Mandela that advocates visibly for coexistence. Nelson Mandela did this after half-a-century of apartheid and decades in prison himself. However, he knew this outreach was the key to creating a partner for the future on the other side.

This reality needs to then play out in practice. How can this be achieved to demonstrate that the vast majority of Palestinian society is ready for coexistence with Israel and vice versa? This is where things like the oft-maligned Seeds of Peace and Abraham Accords come back into play. These are the settings where Israelis and Palestinians can interact in third-party contexts, allowing for the imagination of new possibilities.

A lot of this obligation appears to fall on the weaker side of the conflict, the Palestinians, who already are without a formal state. Ultimately, this is due to the fundamental reality that the greater power does rest with Israel. It will be incumbent on Palestinians to undertake proactive efforts to shift the dynamic in their favor, even if that appears to be unfair. The history of the conflict has demonstrated amply that power and shifting incentives determine the outcomes on the ground.

### Camp David 3

Ultimately, the United States is the main supporter and arms supplier for Israel and is the dominant global power. It will preside over any peace process. It has the requisite influence to bring both sides to the table, in particular Israel. There has to be, and there will be a Camp David 3; there will be no quiet without it. It will happen whether under President Biden, President Trump, or President X.

At this summit, there will need to be a clear timeline for the Palestinian state at the onset with the broad contours defined.

- **Basis of 242 and 338** — The two UN resolutions ending the wars in 1967 and 1973 provide the basis for the shape of a Palestinian state.

- **Demilitarized authority** – During an indeterminate period, the Palestinian state will not be able to have offensive capabilities and instead would have its security guaranteed by a third party.

- **Settlers accepted** – There is no scenario in which Israel will remove all the settlements and settlers, and thus, many of them will remain in place in a final deal.

- **Refugee solution** – Without any right of return, especially related to family reunification, a deal will not be palatable to Palestinian interests; much of the nature of refugee return was outlined in negotiations in Taba (January 2001).

- **Jerusalem option** – The idea that there will be no Palestinian formal presence in Jerusalem in a final status agreement is itself a pipe dream that many Israelis have; there will be a Jerusalem option for the Palestinians.

- **Land swaps** – Given the thorny issue of Jerusalem, settlements, and various security requirements, there will not be a clean and clear border based on UN resolutions 242 and 338, and swaps will have to be numerous.

The above dimensions have all been heavily debated, delineated, and detailed. In prior rounds of discussion, Israeli and Palestinian negotiators have come to aligned terms on most aspects. The challenge is, in fact, not the details but the motivation and American willingness to insist on these contours with the parties, notably Israel.

### Arab Peace Investment Dividend (APID)

Pipe dreams are not enough. Even if the United States is determined, the Palestinians are ready, and the Israelis are convinced, there will need to be extra motivation on the table. Real, tangible, ready-to-go motivation.

If the prior peace moves are a pipe dream, here is the pie-in-the-sky initiative: the Arab Peace Investment Dividend (APID). The APID is a $1 trillion investment fund that will flow directly into the Israeli and Palestinian private sector the day after a peace deal is signed. With a 10-year time horizon, $100 billion will be funded and disbursed year-on-year. It will be the greatest investment dividend per capita in modern history.

The idea is for the APID to be formed immediately as a legal entity with a governance mechanism and for commitments to be binding as of today. In addition to sovereign wealth funds from the Middle East, funds from East Asia (perhaps Temasek) and Europe (particularly Norway) could be brought on board, as could pension funds in North America and development finance institutions (DFIs) more broadly from the West. There is no doubt that these funds could be mobilized and committed with the right political push.

Unlike the Abraham Accords or the Deal of the Century, brought by Jared Kushner and the Trump Administration, this is neither a conceptual dividend nor one that precedes peace. It is only activated upon the acceptance of a broad peace (along the lines of the Arab Peace Initiative). It shows actual skin in the game by global and regional actors in peace. And it demonstrates to Israelis and Palestinians alike the financial upside in a financial world.

However, the APID needs a leader to step up and take ownership. If it were the American president, it would not work. If it were a leader from Saudi Arabia, this would be a game changer.

## WHAT IF THE PIPE DREAMS BURST?

In our world today, bereft of ideas, full of political stagnation and materialistic obsessions, the current conflict may continue unabated, not just in the short term but also in the long run. What is another decade for a crisis that will soon enter its ninth decade? Any number of scenarios illustrate the devastating consequences for those on the ground and the wider region—if not the world—should there not be a resolution. Suffice it to say everyone is aware of these consequences. Yet that has not stopped things to this point.

There are two ways to see world events, especially if one is an institutional leader but also for individuals. Either they occur, or they are shaped. Ultimately, at some level, the outcome is shaped by the decisions of those in power today. The outcome is not set. Destiny may be the provenance of the divine, but it is up to humanity to play its role.

Will you play yours?

# ADDITIONAL RESOURCES

There are innumerable resources on the conflict. Anything listed here does not represent an endorsement. Some of these sources are explicitly biased or even related to the warring factions. They are listed here to enable access to primary information so readers can independently weigh what is accurate or not. All must survey a wider variety of literature and adjust accordingly.

## OVERALL NEWS ON THE REGION

- Yedioth Ahronoth (www.ynetnews.com)
  Widely read daily paper in Israel

- Haaretz (www.haaretz.com)
  Israel's left-leaning publication

- Al Jazeera (www.aljazeera.com)
  Qatar's leading global news platform

- Al Mayadeen (english.almayadeen.net)
  Lebanese pro-'resistance' perspective

- Arab News (www.arabnews.com)
  Saudi's leading English publication

- +972 Magazine (www.972mag.com)
  Israel/Palestine pro-peace publication
- Tabletmag (www.tabletmag.com)
  Jewish magazine on global affairs
- Mondoweiss (mondoweiss.net)
  Anti-Zionist platform on the Middle East
- Electronic Intifada (electronicintifada.net)
  Palestinian diaspora-led outlet

## BOOKS

- *A History of the Modern Middle East* — William Cleveland
- *Middle Eastern Maze: Israel, the Arabs, and the Region 1948-2022* — Itamar Rabinovitch
- *The Ethnic Cleansing of Palestine* — Ilan Pappe
- *Righteous Victims: A History of the Zionist-Arab Conflict, 1881-2001* — Benny Morris
- *The Iron Wall: Israel and the Arab World* — Avi Shlaim
- *Start-up Nation: The Story of Israel's Economic Miracle* — Dan Senor and Saul Singer
- *All That Remains: The Palestinian Villages Occupied and Depopulated by Israel in 1948* — Walid Khalidi
- *The Iron Cage: The Story of the Palestinian Struggle for Statehood* — Rashid Khalidi
- *Rise and Kill First: The Secret History of Israel's Targeted Assassinations* — Ronen Bergman
- *From Beirut to Jerusalem* — Thomas Friedman
- *Pity the Nation: Lebanon at War* — Robert Fisk
- *Hamas: A History from Within* — Azzam Tamimi

- *Black Wave: Saudi Arabia, Iran, and the Forty-Year Rivalry That Unraveled Culture, Religion, and Collective Memory in the Middle East* — Kim Ghattas
- *A History of the Jews* — Paul Johnson

## OTHER RESOURCES

- Council on Foreign Relations
  (www.cfr.org/israeli-palestinian-conflict)
  Overview and background on the conflict

- Security Council Report
  (www.securitycouncilreport.org/un-documents-all)
  All UN resolutions about the conflict

- Carter Center
  (www.cartercenter.org/documents/1435.pdf)
  Summary of key negotiation points before 2002

## SOCIAL MEDIA ON X

X/Twitter is a mess right now. Brilliance and chaos—bystanders will likely be trampled by misinformation and unfriendly fire. However, it is the best place for real-time information from multiple perspectives, including government officials from across the Middle East.

*love thy neighbor*
*as thyself*

# ABOUT THE AUTHOR

Strategist, investor, and writer Taufiq Rahim focuses on the intersection of global geopolitics and transformative technology in a changing world. He first began work in the Middle East in the rural communities of Syria in 2003 and is currently building platforms within the 2040 World nexus.

Over the last two decades, Rahim has driven investment, convened conversations, and forged public and private partnerships across the West and Global South, tackling critical issues from disruptive technology and economic development to geopolitics and global health. He is often cited by the *Financial Times, Washington Post, New York Times, Bloomberg, CNN, CNBC, Al Jazeera, Arab News*, and more.

Rahim is originally from Vancouver, Canada. When not writing, he finds himself equally at home in the sweltering sands of the desert or the fresh powder on the mountain.

www.ingramcontent.com/pod-product-compliance
Lightning Source LLC
Chambersburg PA
CBHW020358130626
46549CB00006B/2333